It's very important for people who make a decision to follow Jesus to understand about the new and wonderful life that they have begun. Steve Legg has excellent communication skills and is very good at explaining truth in a simple yet profound way for all to appreciate and enjoy.

Ishmael – The Glorie Company

If you have recently committed your life to Christ, and you want to learn how to get close to him and stay there, then do yourself a favour and read this book. There are certain things in your life you deserve to get right. Getting out of a straitjacket when you are suspended from the jib of a crane is one of them, and laying good foundations for an eternal relationship with God is another. I wholeheartedly recommend this latest book by Steve Legg.

Russell Boulter – Actor

Steve Legg is truly a man of God. His life, his words, his whole being backs this up. *Firm Foundations* is one of many books that Steve has written and it is simple, easy to understand and will help Christians grow in Jesus.

Bobby Ball – Comedian

There are a lot of people, hundreds of thousands actually, who in the last few years have been seriously considering what it means to love God, follow the teachings of Christ and to be a Christian. Steve Legg in this important publication helps us understand what it means to be a follower of Christ using non-religious language (Jesus was not religious!) and drawing on the wealth of experience he's had as a communicator of the Christian message. Beginning is important, enduring to the end is even more important and this publication will help you do just that.

Gerald Coates – Pioneer

There's a saying in show business, 'Only the truly great entertainers can hold an audience outdoors in Littlehampton when it's raining.' Well coincidentally the last time I worked with Steve Legg was outdoors in Littlehampton and the weather wasn't great. He marched on that day with a kitchen utensil and a straitjacket and went down a storm during a storm. I've always admired people who are able to be entertaining and impart Christian truths without the clunk of 'Uh-oh, here comes the serious bit.' Steve's good at that. He communicates without clunks. Enjoy this book. It's ideal reading material under your umbrella in Littlehampton.

Tim Vine – Comedian

He really is very clever indeed.

Mrs Legg – Steve's mum

This book is a must for anyone who wants to understand more about having 'faith' in God. It will make you laugh and cry as Steve unpacks these ancient truths in a way that only he can.

Martin Smith – Delirious?

Firm Foundations

A Beginner's Guide to Christianity

Steve Legg

Hodder & Stoughton
LONDON SYDNEY AUCKLAND

Copyright © 2003 by Steve Legg

First published in Great Britain in 2003

The right of Steve Legg to be identified as the Author of
the Work has been asserted by him in accordance with the
Copyright, Designs and Patents Act 1988.

10 9 8 7 6 5 4 3 2 1

British Library Cataloguing in Publication Data
A record for this book is available from the British Library

ISBN 0 340 86134 7

Typeset in Bembo by Avon DataSet Ltd,
Bidford-on-Avon, Warwickshire

Printed and bound in Great Britain by Clays Ltd, St Ives, plc

The paper and board used in this paperback are natural recyclable
products made from wood grown in sustainable forests.
The manufacturing processes conform to the environmental
regulations of the country of origin.

Hodder & Stoughton
A Division of Hodder Headline Ltd
338 Euston Road
London NW1 3BH
www.madaboutbooks.com

For Karl.
Hope this helps, mate.

Contents

Foreword

In these days we all suffer from collective amnesia. In spite of all our maps and tracking systems, our lap-tops and palm-tops, our memos and reminders, we forget. Names, birthdays, facts, directions, faces, keys, places and dates. But most of the time we don't care, because we choose not to remember for all we need is NOW.

We live, so the experts tell us, 'in a state of the constant present'. In the eternal now. We expect and demand everything NOW, so if it takes longer than twenty minutes to cook a meal or three days for something to arrive in the post, it can't be worth waiting for. We live life instantly with our instant food and drink, taking pictures on our instant cameras and getting them processed in an hour.

This attitude affects all areas of our lives; our work, our relationships, our pleasures and our pursuits. And for those of us who follow Jesus, our life with God. So we expect everything NOW; holiness, intimacy, dynamic prayer, healing, guidance and perfect churches. And if we haven't got it, we turn to some new theory or strategy, some recently branded and heavily endorsed course to get us where we should be. We rush about from conference to conference overturning stones looking for new solutions. We are always open to try the latest techniques, to listen to the latest ground-shaking message.

What we fail to realise is we are exhibiting exactly the same malaise as our non-Christian society.

For us as Christians to be obsessed with now, with techniques that are shiny and new, is a form of idolatry which our faith encourages us away from. And it does that through rooting us in the past. Our faith owes more to the past than the present; it's not just about now, it's about then. The things that are to be valued in the faith aren't the shiny novelties – they are the overlooked, dusty, rather dulled-through-familiarity truths which have for centuries been everything that everyone who has followed Jesus has needed to know and base their lives on.

My friend Steve Legg is doing nothing new. He is claiming nothing new. He is telling us nothing new. And that's why we need to take notice. You see, the things he writes about have stood the test of time. They are topics which will never be consigned to the sell-by-date basket or out-of-date shelf. In years to come the majority of the hot issues we are preoccupied with will be non-issues. The only time the issues which Steve Legg writes about, in his own engaging and lively way, will not be needed is in the New Heaven and New Earth.

Our amnesia, our forgetfulness, our preoccupation with the here and now, can be cured through rooting ourselves in the Good News of God's work for us in history. To be rooted in this past, to build on these foundations, will save us from ourselves and our misguided generation. For some of you this book will work to repoint your foundations which have not really received any attention for years. For others the foundations might have got flooded and be in danger of subsidence – for you it will pump out what's not needed and set you on solid ground. For some at the beginning of building your house with God, the contents of this book will make your walls straight and your standing firm for the coming years. None of us can fail to be helped. If only everyone would read it.

J. John

Acknowledgments

Thanks to my four children, Jay, Amber, Emmie and Maddie, and especially to my wife Jemma, for putting up with me while I was writing this book, especially during my stressed and grumpy moments when I was trying to meet deadlines.

Thanks to Karl Twort for suggesting the book in the first place following our weekly visit to the Rustington Sports and Social Club, and to Ishy, Bobby, Tim, Russ, Gerald and J. John for their kind words. Thanks as well to Kerry Strotton and Doug Harris for their suggestions, and in particular to David Thatcher, who took the time and trouble to read through an early draft and make lots of useful suggestions.

To my Trustees, Paul, Andy and Jonathan, and all the partners of the Breakout Trust in the UK and farther afield, thanks for believing in me and making this book, and everything else that I do possible. I couldn't do it without you all.

About the Author

Steve Legg is an evangelist, escapologist, author and Director of the Breakout Trust, a UK-based charity committed to communicating the relevance of the Christian faith. This is done through a variety of ways including trickery, mystery, comedy and escapology. Dangerous and daring escapes suspended from cranes or manacled between high-powered jeeps going in opposite directions have brought massive attention to Steve's abilities to draw and entertain large crowds across the world.

As well as entertaining, though, Steve often uses his skills to communicate a powerful message of freedom through Christianity. Steve talks and demonstrates his talents in schools, colleges, universities, pubs, night clubs and out on the streets, from Portland Prison to Canterbury Cathedral – in fact, wherever people are.

Steve travels the length and breadth of the country as well as working in various countries across the world. He has been privileged to work with a whole list of household names and he has appeared on national television on numerous occasions. His impressive list of TV credits include *How 2*, *The Big Breakfast* and *The Disney Club* right through to *Songs of Praise*. In 1995, Steve was part of 'The Cannon and Ball Gospel Show' that toured the

UK. This major tour covered a staggering forty-eight dates across the nation, making it one of the biggest gospel tours ever produced. The show was also the subject of a BBC special documentary, and became the number one best-selling video of its kind.

On top of all this, Steve is also an accomplished presenter, broadcaster and writer. He has written a number of gospel booklets that have been translated into many different languages, as well as penning four paperbacks.

He is married to Jemma and they have four small children, Jay, Amber, Emmie and Maddie. They are all part of Arun Community Church in Littlehampton, West Sussex. Steve is also a member of the Rustington Sports and Social Club and London's prestigious Magic Circle, and is a very proud and active member of the Curry Club.

Introduction

Builder Ray Strank was pleased with the roof tiling he finished on the 27th November 1984. He had spent a few days on the job in Wimbledon, south London, and was delighted with the finished result. But his boss, brother Gordon, was furious when he saw it. Would you believe it? Ray had tiled the wrong house.

The lady in the house, who had been supplying tea for Ray while the work was being done, was as embarrassed as he was. She had assumed that her husband had ordered the work to be done. What a nightmare!

I don't know what your experience of builders is like. I've always been pretty fortunate myself. Indeed, the last such labourer we had in became quite a friend. This was in spite of his constant head-shaking and tut-tutting at the efforts of 'cowboy builders' who had previously attempted work on our humble abode.

Our dear builder, who we'll call Glenn (because that was his name), had the obligatory pencil balanced behind his ear, a lopsided grin and low-slung Levi's. He could talk for England, drank tea by the gallon and seemed to be a world authority on every subject known to mankind. He eventually left our lives after what seemed weeks and I don't think my bank account has ever been the same since.

Jesus must have known a lot of Glenns in his work as a carpenter and would have had a lot of construction experience himself. He would have been genned up on all the tricks of the trade and all the shortcuts. He certainly knew that one of the keys to a really good building was the need for strong foundations. This is a story he told one day:

> Why do you call me, 'Lord, Lord,' and do not do what I say? I will show you what he is like who comes to me and hears my words and puts them into practice. He is like a man building a house, who dug down deep and laid the foundation on rock. When the flood came, the torrent struck that house but could not shake it, because it was well built. But the one who hears my words and does not put them into practice is like a man who built a house on the ground without a foundation. The moment the torrent struck that house, it collapsed and its destruction was complete.
>
> (Luke 6:46–9)

It's a helpful illustration that was probably taken straight off a Palestine building site he had laboured on. In the part of the Middle East where Jesus lived and worked, many of the rivers dried up altogether in the blistering summer months and would have left a sandy bed. Many a person looking for a good site to build a house would have found such an inviting stretch of sand, and would have built there, saving themselves hours of time, toil and sweat. Everything would have been fine until the September rains came, which in turn would have filled the empty river beds once again and completely washed the house away.

Jesus contrasts this foolishness with the man who searched for rock to build his perfect home. You don't need to be a geology expert to know that digging into rock is harder than nice soft sand, and it would have taken much hard graft to have dug the foundations into the rock face. But, of course, eventually the hard work was repaid when the foul winter weather hit and the house stood secure.

Like so many people, the foolish man wanted the easy way out. The thought of digging into rock probably made him sweat just thinking about it. The sand was a much nicer proposition and much less trouble. In our own lives, if I'm really honest, there are easier ways to live than the Christian way. It's certainly not the cushy, easy option. Being a Christian isn't always easy and in many respects it is hard, but ultimately Jesus' way is the best way.

Second, our foolish builder's outlook was somewhat short-sighted. He was only thinking short term, not mid-term and certainly not long term. In his building on the sand he was just thinking of the next six months at the outside. When life was calm, like the weather, everything was okay for him; when things got a little harder, his foundations, or rather the lack of them, were severely tested, and he was left homeless with some serious explaining to do.

In this book I'm going to be attempting to help you put down some strong foundations into your new-found faith, so that it won't remain a weak or unstable faith but instead one that is able to withstand the hard times. I've tried my very best to write the book in a down-to-earth, honest, easy and accessible way, and I've also included a section at the end of each chapter to help you delve a little deeper. Please do take the time and trouble to work your way through these sections and then have a go at memorising the scripture verse I've suggested. I've found that memorising portions of the Bible is a great discipline to get into.

In the story, Jesus was teaching that the Christian way of life would never last unless it was built on a strong foundation – and, of course, the only really firm foundation is Jesus.

So, happy reading. And Glenn, if you're reading this – the cheque's in the post!

Steve Legg
June 2002

1

God

Back of all, above all, before all is God; first in sequential order, above in rank and station, exalted in dignity and honour.

A. W. Tozer

There is no God. All of the wonders around us are accidental. No almighty hand made a thousand stars. They made themselves. No power keeps them on a steady course. The earth spins itself to keep the oceans from falling towards the sun. Infants teach themselves to cry when they are hungry or hurt. A small flower invented itself so that we could extract digitalis for sick hearts.

The earth gave itself day and night, tilted itself so that we get seasons. Without the magnetic poles man would be unable to navigate the trackless oceans of water and air, but they just grew there. Why does snow sit on mountain tops waiting for the warm spring sun to melt it just at the right time for the young crops in farms below to drink? A very lovely accident.

How about the sugar thermostat in the pancreas? It maintains a level of sugar in the blood sufficient for energy.

Without it, all of us would fall into a coma and die. The human heart will beat for seventy to eighty years or more without faltering. How does it get sufficient rest between beats? A kidney will filter poison from the blood and leave good things alone. How does it know one from the other? Who gave the human tongue flexibility to form words, and a brain to understand them, but denied it to the animals?

Who showed a womb how to take the love of two persons and keep splitting a tiny ovum until, in time, a baby would have the proper number of fingers, eyes and ears and hair in the right places, and come into the world when it is strong enough to sustain life? There is no God?

(Jim Bishop, written for the *Miami Herald*)

As ex-nun Maria warbled to the children in the hit musical *The Sound of Music*, 'Let's start at the very beginning. A very good place to start . . .' So here we are, right at the very beginning – with God.

In creation

The Bible from the very first verse onwards makes the assumption that God exists and is very real. He has no beginning and he has no end. He has always been there and always will be there. In Genesis we read: 'In the beginning God created the heavens and the earth' (Genesis 1:1).

Although we can't physically see God, we can see the effects of God all around us – in the wonders of creation, for example. Eugene Crenan, one of the American astronauts who enjoyed the exciting experience of walking on the moon, said with wonder as he looked at our planet from space:'Our world appears big and beautiful, all blue and white! You can see from the Antarctic to the North Pole. The earth looks so perfect. There are no strings to hold it up; there is no fulcrum upon which it rests.'

Contemplating the infinity of time and space, he said he felt as if he were seeing the earth from God's perspective. And it's not just astronauts who talk of the earth as God's handiwork. The Bible tells us, too. Take a look at the first part of Psalm 19:

> The heavens declare the glory of God;
>   the skies proclaim the work of his hands.
> Day after day they pour forth speech;
>   night after night they display knowledge.
> There is no speech or language
>   where their voice is not heard.
> Their voice goes out into all the earth,
>   their words to the ends of the world.
> In the heavens he has pitched a tent for the sun,
>   which is like a bridegroom coming forth from his
>   pavilion,
>   like a champion rejoicing to run his course.
> It rises at one end of the heavens
>   and makes its circuit to the other;
>   nothing is hidden from its heat.
>
> (Psalm 19:1–6)

The New Testament carries this concept further:

> Since what may be known about God is plain to them, because God has made it plain to them. For since the creation of the world God's invisible qualities – his eternal power and divine nature – have been clearly seen, being understood from what has been made, so that men are without excuse.
>
> (Romans 1:19–20)

Paul, the author of this book, makes it clear. No one has an excuse for not believing in God. God has revealed what he is like, in and through creation.

Always there

One of the most regular questions I get asked about God is the old chestnut, 'Who made God?' I always have to admit that the answer's not easy to explain or, for that matter, understand. Basically, the answer's short and sweet. No one. I believe God's always been there and always will be there.

In the eighteenth century the philosopher Jean Jacques Rousseau attempted to describe it like this.

> I know nothing of his having created matter, bodies, spirits or the world. The idea of creation confounds me and surpasses my conception, though I believe as much of it as I am able to conceive. But I know that God has formed the universe and all that exists, in the most consummate order. He is doubtless eternal, but I am incapacitated to conceive an idea of eternity. All that I can conceive is, that he existed before all things, that he exists with them and will exist after them, if they should ever have an end.

Now, the statement that God has always been there and will always be there might be a bit of a strange concept to get our tiny minds around. After all, everything needs to be created. Well yes, that's certainly true for physical things like the chair I'm sitting on at this very minute, or the keyboard that I'm thumping away at to write this book. But the Bible says God is spiritual, not physical. 'He is before all things, and in him all things hold together' (Colossians 1:17).

So it's not outside the realms of possibility to suggest that spiritual beings don't have to obey physical laws, and in fact exist totally outside of these laws. Professor Sir Ghillean Prance, the Director of the Royal Botanical Gardens at Kew in London, said: 'Physical laws came into being because there is a Creator who made them.'

Picturing God

A little boy was working hard on a drawing and his father asked him what he was doing. The reply came back, 'Drawing a picture of God.'

His dad said, 'You can't do that, son. Nobody knows what God looks like.'

But the little boy was undeterred and continued to draw. He looked at his picture with great satisfaction and said, very matter-of-factly, 'They will in a few minutes.'

Now, of course, the mere mention of God can conjure up interesting mental images. When I was at school I always used to have an image of God as an old Father Christmas lookalike strumming a gold harp, with a bushy white beard, going thin on top and wearing a Marks and Spencer nightie.

Others view him as a mysterious, impersonal cosmic 'force', or maybe as a bitter and severe authoritarian sergeant-major type who wants to stop us having fun. For others he's viewed as a kind of celestial Jimmy Saville, floating around heaven 'fixing it' for people in times of trouble.

Are any of these views accurate, I wonder? Of course, the Bible doesn't have any pictures or photographs of God, but it does say that people were made in the 'image' and 'likeness' of God (Genesis 1:26). This kind of description is given the very technical name of 'anthropomorphism', which is taken from *anthropos*, 'man', and *morphe*, which means 'shape'. So, in one sense, God looks like you and me. For ease of communication we usually talk of God as a father, though of course male and femaleness are both part of God's character.

The American best-selling author Philip Yancey described God like this:

People grow up with all sorts of notions of what God is like. They see God as an Enemy, or a Policeman, or even an Abusive Parent. Or perhaps they do not see God at all and only hear his silence. Because of Jesus, however, we no longer have to wonder how God feels or what he is like. When in doubt, we can look at Jesus to correct our blurry vision.

Father God

The emphasis changes slightly in the New Testament, where God is described as 'Father'. This is so important, because God's not just a strange religious force or power, he's a person who has character and feelings and is a personal God who wants to get to know people.

In biblical days a Jewish father ruled, provided and cared for his family. Paul, an important New Testament church leader, described Christians as adopted children of God, that God had bought so we could become his children (Galatians 4:5). Paul went on to encourage us to call God 'Abba'. I'm not talking about the 1970s Swedish super-group but instead the most intimate Jewish family word, literally 'Daddy'. That's a great picture of God, a heavenly dad who loves and cares, and wants the best for us, not just in our 'spiritual' lives but in every aspect of our existence: physically, emotionally and spiritually. With God you get the whole package.

Everywhere

The Bible teaches that God is everywhere. The technical name for God being everywhere is 'omnipresence', a word that I'm sure often crops up at the Christian Scrabble Club, if such an organisation exists. If God is the Lord of time and space, because he created it, then time and space have no restrictions on God.

He is everywhere, all of the time, but can act in different ways as he sees fit.

A man once asked God how long a million years was to him. God replied, 'It's just like a single second of your time, my child.'

So the man asked, 'And what about a million pounds?'

The Lord replied, 'To me, it's just like a single penny.'

So the man made some quick mental calculations and said, 'Well, Lord, could I have one of your pennies?'

And God said, 'Certainly, my child. Just a second . . .'

There is nowhere in the universe that we can escape God's presence. That is so awesome and powerful. King David summed up God's omnipresence:

> Where can I go from your Spirit?
>> Where can I flee from your presence?
> If I go up to the heavens, you are there;
>> if I make my bed in the depths, you are there.
> If I rise on the wings of the dawn,
>> if I settle on the far side of the sea,
> even there your hand will guide me,
>> your right hand will hold me fast.
>
>> (Psalm 139:7–10)

All-knowing

'Omniscience'. Another strange word that simply means that God knows everything – past, present and future, the good, the bad and the ugly! John tells us: 'For God is greater than our hearts, and he knows everything' (1 John 3:20). God knows what has happened, all things that happen, and all things that might happen. Once again, that is absolutely mind-blowing.

For example, God knows how many hairs are on your head. He knows how many grains of sand are on Littlehampton beach, five minutes' walk from my house. He knows how many blades of grass are in your back garden. He knows the answer without having to count them. He knows everything at once, without having to scratch his head and rack his brains for the answer.

Powerful

Right. Brace yourself for another, and I promise the last, 'O' word – 'omnipotence'. It means power. The word itself is made up of two Latin words, *omni*, which as you've probably guessed by now means 'all', and *potens*, which means 'powerful'. God is all-powerful. He can do whatever he wants, whenever he wants. There are no restrictions whatsoever on the power or sovereignty of God.

The Bible tells us that nothing is too hard for God. Jeremiah, a great and faithful prophet from the Old Testament, wrote: 'Ah, Sovereign LORD, you have made the heavens and the earth by your great power and outstretched arm. Nothing is too hard for you' (Jeremiah 32:17).

In the New Testament, an angel turned up in Mary's kitchen to tell her that she was going to be pregnant. A pretty impossible thing if you're a virgin. The angel told her that 'nothing is impossible with God' (Luke 1:37). Jesus said: 'with God all things are possible' (Matthew 19:26). You really don't need to be a Bible scholar with a string of letters after your name to understand what the Bible is saying here. In a word, or rather in five words: nothing is impossible for God.

Dependable

Now of course, the view we have of our human father has a large influence on our view of our Heavenly Father. Even the best, most well-meaning father will let his children down on occasions. That's the very nature of being human and fallible. But God, our heavenly dad, will never let us down.

Someone once said God will never get disillusioned with us, because he never had any illusions in the first place. He knows everything about us and still loves us to bits: 'Every good and perfect gift is from above, coming down from the Father of the heavenly lights, who does not change like shifting shadows' (James 1:17).

We need to understand that God is completely and utterly dependable. If we give him our all, by giving him our lives – lock, stock and barrel – he'll never let us down. In fact, he'll go out of his way to look after us:

This poor man called, and the LORD heard him:
    he saved him out of all his troubles.
The angel of the LORD encamps around those who fear him,
    and he delivers them.
Taste and see that the LORD is good;
    blessed is the man who takes refuge in him.

                    (Psalm 34:6–8)

We need to believe that God knows best. His wisdom is mentioned throughout the Bible. A man called Job went through a particularly tough time in the Old Testament, but ultimately Job knew that God knew best. Read what he said about God's wisdom on two different occasions: 'His wisdom is profound, his power is vast' (Job 9:4), and then, 'To God belong wisdom and power; counsel and understanding are his' (Job 12:13).

In our lives today, God knows what's best for us. There's a great example of this in the encouraging words of Paul to the Christians in Rome: 'And we know that in all things God works for the good of those who love him, who have been called according to his purpose' (Romans 8:28).

Best friend

Friends look out for each other. They watch each other's backs. God's like that too:

'Because he loves me,' says the LORD, 'I will rescue him;
   I will protect him, for he acknowledges my name.
He will call upon me, and I will answer him;
   I will be with him in trouble,
   I will deliver him and honour him.'

(Psalm 91:14–15)

Many years ago, a famous American actor was the guest of honour at a very upmarket garden party. During the afternoon he received many requests to recite favourite excerpts from various literary classics. An elderly Christian minister who happened to be there asked the actor to recite the Twenty-Third Psalm. The actor agreed on the condition that afterwards the minister would also read it. The actor's rendition was beautifully read with great dramatic emphasis and he received a long round of applause. Next, it was the minister's turn. His voice was rough and hoarse from many years of preaching, and his diction was far from polished. But when he finished there was not a dry eye at the party. When someone asked the actor what made the difference, he replied, 'I know the psalm, but he knows the Shepherd.'

It's really quite staggering that the King of Kings and Lord of Lords wants to have a very special friendship with us. Christians believe God is infinite – in other words, greater than anything he has made – but also personal. He's interested in us. No other religion has a God like that. The New Testament book of James tells us: 'And the scripture was fulfilled that says, "Abraham believed God, and it was credited to him as righteousness," and he was called God's friend' (James 2:23). That's the relationship God wants with every one of his children – not to be a distant acquaintance in a far-off place, but instead your very best friend who'll look after you and who wants the very best for you.

Gentle corrector

My three-year-old daughter loves trying to ride her big brother's skateboard. But I don't let Emmie demonstrate her skateboarding skills out in the road by herself. It's not because I want to spoil her fun, but because I love her and don't want her to get hurt falling off, or being run over by the number 47 bus. It's the same with our relationship with God. He's not a cosmic killjoy who wants to stop us having fun. Neither does he want to beat us over the head with a big stick when we step out of line. That's not the nature of God.

The book of Hebrews, which was written to Jews struggling in their faith, says this about God's correction and discipline:

> 'My son, do not make light of the Lord's discipline,
>   and do not lose heart when he rebukes you,
> because the Lord disciplines those he loves,
>   and he punishes everyone he accepts as a son.'

Endure hardship as discipline; God is treating you as sons. For what son is not disciplined by his father? If you are not disciplined (and everyone undergoes discipline), then you are illegitimate children and not true sons. Moreover, we have all had human fathers who disciplined us and we respected them for it. How much more should we submit to the Father of our spirits and live! Our fathers disciplined us for a little while as they thought best; but God disciplines us for our good, that we may share in his holiness. No discipline seems pleasant at the time, but painful. Later on, however, it produces a harvest of righteousness and peace for those who have been trained by it.

(Hebrews 12:5–11)

Quite simply, God knows what's best for us.

Lover and forgiver

Take a moment to read, then reread and mull over the words of King David in the book of Psalms:

> Praise the LORD, O my soul,
>   and forget not all his benefits –
> who forgives all your sins
>   and heals all your diseases,
> who redeems your life from the pit
>   and crowns you with love and compassion,
> who satisfies your desires with good things
>   so that your youth is renewed like the eagle's.
> The LORD works righteousness
>   and justice for all the oppressed.
> He made known his ways to Moses,
>   his deeds to the people of Israel:
> The LORD is compassionate and gracious,
>   slow to anger, abounding in love.
> He will not always accuse,
>   nor will he harbour his anger for ever;
> he does not treat us as our sins deserve
>   or repay us according to our iniquities.
> For as high as the heavens are above the earth,
>   so great is his love for those who fear him;
> as far as the east is from the west,
>   so far has he removed our transgressions from us.
> As a father has compassion on his children,
>   so the LORD has compassion on those who fear him.
>   (Psalm 103:2–13)

God promises never to hold our sins against us, as long as we genuinely and sincerely ask for his forgiveness. Whatever you've said, done or thought that is wrong, no sin is too bad for God to forgive. Isn't that mind-blowing? ' "Come now, let us reason together," says the LORD. "Though your sins are like scarlet, they shall be as white as snow; though they are red as crimson, they shall be like wool" ' (Isaiah 1:18). How about that for unconditional love?

Knowing God

In conclusion, in God we have a wonderful Heavenly Father who desires to be involved intimately with us and everything we do — not just the Christian parts of our lives, but involved with every aspect of them. God made that possible by coming to the earth as a human, in the form of Jesus, over two thousand years ago.

There is an ancient tale from India about a young man who was seeking God. He went to a wise old sage for help. 'How can I find God?' he asked the old man. The old man took him to a nearby river and they waded into the deep water. Soon the water was up just under their chins. Suddenly the old man seized the young man by the neck and pushed him under the water. He held the young man down until he was flailing the water in desperation. Another minute and he may well have drowned. They struggled out of the river, the young man coughing water from his lungs and still gasping for air. Reaching the bank he asked the man indignantly, 'What did that have to do with my finding God?'

The old man asked him quietly, 'While you were under the water, what did you want more than anything else?'

The young man thought for a moment and then answered, 'I wanted air. I wanted air more than anything else!'

The old man replied, 'When you want God as much as you wanted air, you will find him.'

Delving deeper

What do we know about God?
1 Genesis 1:27
2 Psalm 34:8
3 Micah 7:18
4 Acts 17:26–7
5 Colossians 1:16

What are some of the characteristics of God?
1 2 Chronicles 7:3
2 Job 42:2
3 Psalm 78:35–9
4 Psalm 90:2
5 Psalm 91:1–3
6 Psalm 139:7–10
7 Isaiah 6:3
8 John 4:24
9 John 10:3
10 Philippians 4:19
11 Hebrews 4:13
12 Hebrews 12:5–11
13 1 John 4:7–9
14 1 John 4:16

Memory verses

> In the beginning you laid the foundations of the earth,
>   and the heavens are the work of your hands.
> They will perish, but you remain;
>   they will all wear out like a garment.
> Like clothing you will change them
>   and they will be discarded.
> But you remain the same,
>   and your years will never end.
>
>   (Psalm 102:25–7)

2
Sin

Sin pays – but it pays in remorse, regret, and failure.

Billy Graham

In the Australian bush you'll often find growing a little plant called the sundew. It has a slender stem and tiny round leaves fringed with hairs that glisten with bright drops of liquid as delicate as fine dew. It looks stunning, but it's very bad news to any insect that dares to go anywhere near it. For while its attractive clusters of red, white and pink blossoms are totally harmless, the leaves are deadly. The shiny moisture on each leaf is sticky and will hold prisoner any insect that touches it. The struggle to get free makes things even worse, for the frantic movements of the insect cause the leaves to close even more tightly. This innocent-looking plant actually feeds upon its victims if they do not get out fast.

That true example from nature is a perfect picture of 'sin'. It all seems so innocent, exciting and attractive at the time, but it is so easy to get caught by it and even destroyed by its consequences. The Oxford English Dictionary defines sin as 'the breaking of divine or moral law, especially by a conscious act'. I guess the Bible would take the dictionary definition even further, because the Scriptures see sin not just as wrong acts, such as murder or adultery, but also wrong thoughts and attitudes.

The Ten Commandments are probably the most obvious example. The complete list is in Exodus chapter 20, but here's an example of what I mean: 'You shall not covet your neighbour's house. You shall not covet your neighbour's wife, or his manservant or maidservant, his ox or donkey, or anything that belongs to your neighbour' (Exodus 20:17). Of course 'covet' means 'earnestly desire', and it's clear that wrong thoughts, attitudes and desires are sin.

In the New Testament Jesus preached a famous sermon on a hillside near Capernaum in Galilee that has become known as the 'Sermon on the Mount'. Bible scholars tell us the 'sermon' probably covered a few days of preaching, so let's take a few minutes to look at a couple of profound points Jesus made.

'But I tell you that anyone who is angry with his brother will be subject to judgment' (Matthew 5:22). Moses said in the Ten Commandments that murder was wrong, but Jesus was saying that anger was wrong too. Anger is contrary to God's command to love one another.

'But I tell you that anyone who looks at a woman lustfully has already committed adultery with her in his heart' (Matthew 5:28). Once again, it's a heart attitude that does the damage. The Old Testament said it was wrong to have sex with someone who was not your own spouse; now Jesus was taking it even further by saying that the desire to have sex with someone other than your spouse is wrong. It is mental adultery and is also sin.

How sin affected humankind

We all sin. But we're not sinners because we sin; we sin because we are sinners. We sin in the things that we all do, say and think that are wrong, and it breaks God's heart.

When God created the world he made it perfect: 'God saw all that he had made, and it was very good' (Genesis 1:31). He'd made light, sky and water, land and seas, sun, moon and stars, fish and birds, animals and man and woman. It was perfect. God also made angels and they were good too, but we know that at some point some of these angels rebelled against God. Throughout history these evil angels who sinned against God have been known as demons, and the head of the demons is the devil, Satan, a Hebrew name that means 'adversary'. Through Satan, sin came into the world and affected the whole human race.

It would have been so easy for God to have created people as robots, programmed to automatically love him and obey his every whim. Instead, God made the first people, Adam and Eve, with free will, so they could choose to obey or disobey, love or reject him. The choice was theirs, and this is where the first sin came from:

> Now the serpent was more crafty than any of the wild animals the LORD God had made. He said to the woman, 'Did God really say, "You must not eat from any tree in the garden"?' The woman said to the serpent, 'We may eat fruit from the trees in the garden, but God did say, "You must not eat fruit from the tree that is in the middle of the garden, and you must not touch it, or you will die." ' 'You will not surely die,' the serpent said to the woman. 'For God knows that when you eat of it your eyes will be opened, and you will be like God, knowing good and evil.'
>
> When the woman saw that the fruit of the tree was good for food and pleasing to the eye, and also desirable for gaining wisdom, she took some and ate it. She also gave some to her husband, who was with her, and he ate it. Then the eyes of both of them were opened, and they realised they were naked; so they sewed fig leaves together and made coverings for themselves.
>
> (Genesis 3:1–7)

It was Satan, in the form of the serpent, who tempted Eve. In eating the forbidden fruit, Adam and Eve were disobeying God. They did exactly the one and only thing God told them explicitly not to do. They also sinned through not being content with what God had given them. They were living in paradise, yet they still wanted more. In the words of the great church leader Paul, at that moment in human history 'sin entered the world through one man' (Romans 5:12). They were banished from the garden for ever and God placed mighty angels with flaming swords at Eden's gates. The rest is history.

Satan and evil

Satan is called 'the prince and power of the air' and the 'god of this world'. We can see his hand in much of the evil that is perpetrated in our world today. Satan sinned before Adam and Eve, and indeed was the originator of sin. As well as tempting Eve to sin in Eden (Genesis 3:1–6), he also tempted Jesus to sin in the wilderness (Matthew 4:1–11). It's Satan and his demons that attempt to make people reject Jesus and turn away from God. They are totally and utterly evil and their tactics include:

1 Murder – Psalm 106:37
2 Temptation – Matthew 4:1–11
3 Snatching away the word of God – Matthew 13:19
4 Lies – John 8:44
5 Blinding people to the gospel – 2 Corinthians 4:4
6 Keeping people in bondage – Galatians 4:8
7 Persecution – Revelation 2:10
8 Deception – Revelation 12:9
9 Accusations – Revelation 12:10

Paul urged the church in Ephesus to be ready for attacks from Satan and demons by donning armour so that they could take their stand against the devil's schemes. Paul reminded them that their struggle was not against flesh and blood, but against the rulers, against the authorities, against the powers of this dark world and against the spiritual forces of evil in the heavenly realms:

> Stand firm then, with the belt of truth buckled round your waist, with the breastplate of righteousness in place, and with your feet fitted with the readiness that comes from the gospel of peace. In addition to all this, take up the shield of faith, with which you can extinguish all the flaming arrows of the evil one. Take the helmet of salvation and the sword of the Spirit, which is the word of God.
>
> (Ephesians 6:14–17)

Paul was saying that truth, righteousness, a readiness to share the gospel, faith, salvation and the word of God would help us stand our ground against evil. Demons will try everything they can to turn people away from God and to stop a Christian's walk with God. But don't worry, you don't need to carry buckets of holy water or a ten-foot crucifix around with you, or cloves of garlic stuffed in your pockets to thwart evil powers. Jesus has given us the armour we need and the authority to fight evil, through what he achieved through his life, death and resurrection: 'Submit yourselves, then, to God. Resist the devil, and he will flee from you' (James 4:7). It's true that Satan and his demons are currently very active in our world, but we know that with the power of the Holy Spirit in our lives we can resist him, and he will run away from us. He doesn't stand a chance.

Original sin

A quick story for you, so I hope you're sitting comfortably. Once upon a time a scorpion, being a very poor swimmer, asked a turtle to carry him on its back across the river.

'Are you mad?' exclaimed the turtle. 'You'll sting me while I'm swimming and I'll drown.'

'My dear turtle,' laughed the scorpion, 'If I were to sting you, you would drown and I'd go down with you. Now where is the logic in that?'

'You're right,' cried the turtle. 'Hop on.'

The scorpion climbed aboard and halfway across the river gave the turtle a huge sting. As they both sank to the bottom, the turtle said, 'Do you mind if I ask you something? You said there is no logic in your stinging me. Why did you do it?'

'It has nothing to do with logic,' the drowning scorpion replied. 'It's just my nature.'

Original sin is a fairly familiar concept to many, though I personally prefer the term 'inherited sin'. I wouldn't want to offend the purists, so I'll stick to 'original' to keep them happy. Quite simply, the concept means we all sin, because we have inherited it from Adam. In other words, it's in our nature to sin.

Look again at the words of Paul: 'Therefore, just as sin entered the world through one man, and death through sin, and in this way death came to all men, because all sinned' (Romans 5:12). Paul makes it crystal clear. Through the sin of Adam we all sin. It's almost as though we're programmed to sin – there's nothing we can really do about it. No one ever taught me to sin, I took to it like a duck to water. I remember all too easily times as a child when I lied, covered up and blamed my little brother if things got broken or damaged. My parents never sat me down and taught me how to do wrong – it just came very naturally. It's exactly the same for all of us. We're all in the same sinking boat. The only person who can save us is a Saviour.

Temptation

It was Oscar Wilde who said, 'I can resist everything except temptation.' We're not tempted because we're evil, we're tempted because we're human, and it's something that we'll all struggle with through all of our Christian lives. It's important to recognise that temptation doesn't come from God. We've already read that all bad things come from Satan, so let's be straight about that from the start. Jesus was tempted: 'For we do not have a high priest who is unable to sympathise with our weaknesses, but we have one who has been tempted in every way, just as we are – yet was without sin' (Hebrews 4:15). So it's clear that Jesus faced temptation, but he never gave in to it. And so it's clear that temptation doesn't inevitably lead to sin.

I know, because I've spoken to other blokes about it, that as far as men go, most of us are tempted in the areas of money, sex and power – or, put another way, girls, gold and glory. I know personally I'm constantly battling in those three areas. But of course, it's not just men who get tempted. I wouldn't want you thinking that men somehow face bigger temptations than women. Though we might face different temptations, we all get tempted – both men and women in equal measure. Whichever sex we might be, we need to remember that it's not a sin to be tempted. Sin is when we give in to the temptation.

But the good news is that we're not alone. Jesus knows how we all struggle from time to time with temptation, and he wants to help. The New Testament gives us some helpful ways of resisting temptation:

1 Recognise it. Be aware that Satan wants to tempt you. Of course, you can't stop a seagull flying over your head, but you can stop it nesting there. Be ready and see it coming.

2 Be humble. In our own strength we're pretty feeble, but in God's strength we can face up to anything. Put on your armour (Ephesians 6), admit your weaknesses, and fight each battle a day at a time.

3 Temptation isn't sin. Temptation doesn't have to lead to sin, so don't feel you're a lousy Christian if you're always getting tempted. Relax, that's perfectly normal. James wrote these words to Christians living throughout the Mediterranean:

'Then, after desire has conceived, it gives birth to sin; and sin, when it is full-grown, gives birth to death' (James 1:15). He was urging the Jewish Christians to stop a temptation before it gets too strong to stop it from turning into sin. They're certainly wise words that we'd all do well to take seriously on board.

4 Use the Bible. When Jesus was tempted in the wilderness he overcame Satan's temptations by quoting Scriptures at him (Matthew 4). Read the Bible, memorise important Scriptures and quote them out loud when you're feeling tempted. It really does work.

5 Avoid it. God will give us a way out: 'No temptation has seized you except what is common to man. And God is faithful; he will not let you be tempted beyond what you can bear. But when you are tempted, he will also provide a way out so that you can stand up under it' (1 Corinthians 10:13). Sometimes that way out is for us to be sensible and avoid it in the first place. We'd all be stupid if we admitted sin wasn't fun. Of course it is, that's why we enjoy doing it so much. But if we're to grow in God, we know it's wrong, so let's avoid it as much as we can. That might mean avoiding certain books, magazines, websites, TV programmes and movies. It could mean avoiding certain people and situations. Whatever it might be for you, avoid it as much as you can, the moment the temptation arrives.

We all sin

The Bible makes it clear from cover to cover that mankind is in essence sinful: 'All have turned aside, they have together become corrupt; there is no one who does good, not even one' (Psalm 14:3). A mighty wise king called Solomon said: 'there is no one who does not sin' (1 Kings 8:46).

Paul ruffled a few feathers when he attempted to show that everyone, both Jew and Greek, was equally guilty of sin: 'What shall we conclude then? Are we any better? Not at all! We have already made the charge that Jews and Gentiles alike are all under sin. As it is written:"There is no one righteous, not even one" ' (Romans 3:9–10). He continued his argument: 'for all have sinned and fall short of the glory of God' (Romans 3:23). However we see ourselves or attempt to compare ourselves with others, we're all the same in the eyes of God.

A true story for you. A large prosperous church did tremendous work with the needy in the heart of inner-city London. They saw some outstanding conversions with thieves, burglars and so on becoming Christians through their work. One Sunday morning during Communion the minister saw a former burglar kneeling beside a high court judge. This man was the very same judge who had sent the burglar to jail, where he had served seven years. After his release this burglar had become a Christian. Yet, as they knelt there, the judge and the former convict, neither one seemed to be aware of the other.

After the service, the judge was walking home with the minister and said to him, 'Did you notice who was kneeling beside me at the Communion rail this morning?'

'Yes,' he replied, 'but I didn't know that you noticed.'

The two walked along in silence for a few more moments, and then the judge said, 'What an amazing example of God's grace.'

The minister nodded in agreement. 'Yes, what a marvellous example of grace.'

Then the judge said, 'But to whom do you refer?'

And the minister said, 'Why, to the conversion of the burglar.'

The judge said, 'But I wasn't referring to him. I was thinking of myself.'

The minister was surprised, and replied, 'You were thinking of yourself? I don't understand.'

'Yes,' the judge answered, 'it didn't cost that burglar much to get converted when he came out of jail. He had nothing but a history of crime behind him, and when he saw Jesus as his

Saviour he knew there was hope for him. And he knew how much he needed that help. But look at me. I was taught from earliest infancy to live as a gentleman; that my word was to be my bond; that I was to say my prayers, go to church, take Communion and so on. I went through Oxford, took my degrees, was called to the bar and eventually became a judge. Nothing but the grace of God could have caused me to admit that I was a sinner on a level with that burglar. It took much more grace to forgive me for all my pride and self-deception, to get me to admit that I was no better in the eyes of God than that convict that I had sent to prison.'

What sin does

Sin is destructive and does many things. Because of the disobedience of Eve and then Adam in Eden at the start of human history, we have become separated from God. When they ate the fruit from the tree of knowledge, the one thing God had told them not to do, their rebellion resulted in total banishment from Eden. Their perfect relationship with God was broken. This separation from God is a consequence of sin.

Sin ties us up because it puts us in bondage. I often use escapology as a very visual illustration of how sin stops us being free. The author of Hebrews didn't use a straitjacket to illustrate this point. Instead, he used powerful words: 'Since the children have flesh and blood, he too shared in their humanity so that by his death he might destroy him who holds the power of death – that is, the devil – and free those who all their lives were held in slavery by their fear of death' (Hebrews 2:14–15). Sin stops people from being really free and the men, women, boys and girls that God intended them to be.

Sin is dangerous. During the Second World War two shells fell close to a house near the scene of the conflict in France. The owner decided to keep them as a souvenir. After polishing them, he put them near his fireplace. Years later he showed these interesting objects to a friend who had dropped in. They were enjoying a cup of coffee together when the visitor was suddenly struck by a horrible thought. 'What if they're still loaded?' he asked, while trying to stay calm. Being something of an expert in such matters, he quickly examined the shells. 'Get them away from the heat of the fire immediately. They're as deadly as the day they were made,' he shouted. Without realising it, for years the man and his family had been in danger. Sin is just like that. It is dangerous and to be avoided at all costs.

The unforgivable sin

All sins can be forgiven except one. Jesus said: 'Whoever blasphemes against the Holy Spirit will never be forgiven; he is guilty of an eternal sin' (Mark 3:29). Jesus' words are repeated in Matthew 12:31–2 and also in Luke 12:10. When I became a Christian at the age of thirteen and read these strong words I was terrified that I had committed the unforgivable sin by mistake and was going to burn in hell! I guess I'm not alone, so let me unpack these words.

First, let's look at the context in which Jesus was making the comments, and to whom. He was addressing his comments to Pharisees, a group of religious people who took the Scriptures and attempted to apply them to the law. For a long time they'd been watching Jesus very carefully and had witnessed incredible miracles and even exorcisms. Jesus was so pure he made the Pharisees feel dirty, and one day they couldn't stand it any more. Something inside them snapped and they shouted a torrent of abuse at him. Their criticisms of his ministry were far from tactful: 'He is possessed by Beelzebub! By the prince of demons he is driving out demons' (Mark 3:22).

The Pharisees knew who Jesus was, and that the Holy Spirit was working through him in astonishing ways, yet they still deliberately and maliciously rejected these facts and instead attributed the work of the Holy Spirit to Beelzebub – Satan.

That's serious stuff. They were committing a sin that was so terrible it would never be forgiven. The unforgivable sin is a persistent and deliberate hardening of the heart towards the ways of God, holding Jesus in utter contempt and crediting the work of God to Satan. That's what these men were doing.

Don't worry, you can't commit it by accident, so don't panic. I would suggest that if you're genuinely worried that you've committed the unforgivable sin, then that concern in itself almost certainly means that you haven't.

When Christians sin

If you're a Christian and you sin, you're forgiven. It really is as simple as that. 'Therefore, there is now no condemnation for those who are in Christ Jesus, because through Christ Jesus the law of the Spirit of life set me free from the law of sin and death' (Romans 8:1). When Jesus died he paid the punishment our sins – past, present and future – deserve. There is no sin that you will ever commit that has not already been included in Christ's death. Much more of that wonderful news in the next chapter.

When Christians sin it upsets God. Of course he still loves us, but we upset our heavenly dad. I'm sure most of us without too much trouble can think of times when our parents, partners or children have upset us. But that doesn't make us stop loving them (I hope!). It's the same with God. When we consistently sin I do believe it affects our relationship with God as well as affecting the effectiveness of our Christian lives. Paul said that if Christians continually sin they become 'slaves' to sin. You can read his exact words in Romans 6:16.

For the Christian, sinning doesn't condemn us – but continuing to sin is a different matter. A visitor at a lake asked an old fisherman who was sitting there, 'If I fell into the water, would I drown?' It was a strange way of asking how deep the water was, but the fisherman had a clever answer up his sleeve.

'No,' he said. 'Falling into the water doesn't drown anybody. It's staying under it that does.'

I hope this chapter hasn't been too depressing and hasn't left you with an urge to stick your head in the oven and turn the gas on, to end it all. Sin is a serious business, but God didn't leave us to fight it by ourselves. Some wonderful good news comes in Chapter 3, so please do stick with it. But let me leave you with a powerful story from around AD 400.

When Chrysostom was arrested, the Roman emperor sought to make the famous Greek Christian deny his faith. But he was unsuccessful. So the emperor discussed with his advisors what they could do to this prisoner.

'Shall I put him in a dungeon?' the emperor asked.

'No,' one of his counsellors replied, 'for he'll be glad to go. He longs for the quietness where he can delight in the mercies of his God.'

'Then he shall be executed!' said the emperor.

'No,' came the answer, 'for he'll be glad to die. He declares that in the event of death, he will be in the presence of the Lord.'

'Well, what shall we do then?' the ruler asked.

The counsellor replied, 'There's only one thing that will cause him pain. Make him sin. He's afraid of nothing but sin.'

Delving deeper

Where did Satan come from?
1 Isaiah 14:12–14
2 Ezekiel 28:11–19
3 Colossians 1:16
4 Revelation 12:7–10

What is sin?
1 Isaiah 53:6
2 John 16:9
3 Romans 2:12–14
4 Romans 14:23

What does sin do?
1 Isaiah 59:2
2 John 8:34
3 Romans 6:23
4 2 Thessalonians 1:6–10
5 Hebrews 6:1

Memory verse

If we confess our sins, he is faithful and just and will forgive
us our sins and purify us from all unrighteousness.

(1 John 1:9)

3

Jesus

I can't believe in Christianity but I think Jesus was a wonderful man.

Billy Connolly

A story was once told of a certain king who was very rich. His power was known throughout the world, but deep down he was very unhappy as he wanted to share his life with someone special. Without a queen, his vast palace was empty.

One day, while riding through the streets of a small village, he saw a beautiful peasant girl. She was so lovely the king instantly fell head over heels in love with her. He wanted her more than anything he had ever desired. Every day, he would ride by her house in the hope of catching a glimpse of her.

He wondered how he might win her love. His first plan was to draw up a royal decree and require her to be brought before him to become the queen of the land. But as he thought about it, he realised that she was a subject and would be forced to obey. He could never be certain that he had won her love.

Then he said to himself, 'I shall call on her in person. I will dress in my finest royal robes, wear my diamond rings, my silver sword, my shiny black boots, and my most colourful tunic. I will overwhelm her and sweep her off her feet to become my bride.' But as he pondered the idea, he knew that he would always wonder whether she had married him for the riches and power he could give her.

Finally, he realised what he must do. He would take off his royal robes. He would go to the village and become one of the peasants. He would work and suffer with them. He would actually become a peasant. This he did. And he eventually won his wife.

And, of course, this was God's plan to win humankind. God became one of us, by wrapping himself up in human form as Jesus. Jesus was God in a body. Even though we didn't deserve it, Jesus came to mend the broken relationship between God and people that had been ruined by sin.

The predictions

The birth and life of Jesus were prophesied hundreds of years before, as was his mission – to give his life for the whole world so that people could know God personally. Here are just a few of the things said about him; please do bear in mind the dates that they were said, and the pinpoint accuracy of these predictions.

In 750 BC a prophet called Micah told of a special man from the family of David coming from a small town called Bethlehem (Micah 5:2–5). The only snag is that the parents chosen for the task, Mary and Joseph, who incidentally were both descendants of King David, lived in Nazareth, some 80 miles due north of Bethlehem. Then a special decree from Rome required them to go to Joseph's home town, which happened to be Bethlehem, just as the baby was about to be born. They probably didn't realise that through following the tedious and inconvenient rules of a taxation census ordered by a pagan empire they were fulfilling God's plan.

Jeremiah prophesied a chilling prediction around 600 BC

when he foretold Rachel 'mourning and weeping' for the dead children. Rachel was buried at Bethlehem, and this fulfilment came to pass during the horrific slaughter of the babies and toddlers in Bethlehem following the birth of Jesus.

Fifty years later, in 550 BC, the prophet Isaiah spoke of a virgin giving birth to a son who would be called Immanuel, which means 'God with us' (Isaiah 7:14). Jesus was born of a virgin over five hundred years later. Isaiah also said that Jesus would live in both Galilee and Nazareth and that his birth would be announced by an Elijah-like herald. This person turned out to be John the Baptist, a cousin of Jesus, who challenged people to prepare for the coming Messiah (Isaiah 40:3–5).

And those are just three of the 322 different Old Testament predictions concerning Jesus. I'm told that using the laws of compound probability, say you'd had the foresight to wager just £1 on each of those prophecies coming true through one man, at one time in history, your final winnings would be a staggering:

£840,000,000,000,000,000,000,000,000,000,000,000,000, 000,000,000,000,000,000,000,000,000,000,000,000,000, 000,000,000,000,000,000,000,000,000.

In other words, you probably wouldn't have to worry about money for a while. And yes, every single one of those prophecies was historically fulfilled in Jesus. They really did happen.

The early days

Cast your minds back to your carefree schooldays and the happy memories of the annual Christmas nativity play. Without too much trouble you should remember that the story began when Jesus' mum, Mary, had a visit from an angel. All of a sudden and quite unexpectedly, this young teenage girl found out that she was pregnant. In those days as an unmarried mother she would have been shunned by society. She could have been thrown into prison or even murdered. To make matters even worse, she heard the surprise news not from a friendly doctor but from an angel, called Gabriel, who suddenly appeared in her kitchen.

Gabriel told Mary that she was going to become a mother, and that her baby would be the Son of God. How Mary grasped the significance of this announcement is just too staggering for words. I mean, first, she was a virgin about to give birth. That was pretty jaw-dropping in itself. But even more astonishing, the child she was to give birth to would be a king. And it didn't end there, as next she heard that this 'king' was to be the Son of God! But, the angel reassured her, she wasn't to be afraid as God was with her in these unusual circumstances, and her child was to be very special indeed.

Poor old Joseph, the earthly father of Jesus, took the news rather differently from Mary. Just think how this upright citizen felt when he discovered that his teenage bride-to-be was expecting a baby. His reputation would have been in tatters, and he could well have suffered violent attacks for damaging the honour of his fiancée's family.

It was an awkward situation, to say the least, and would have made compulsive viewing if it was a scene played out in *EastEnders*. The tabloids would have had a field day with the news. Just imagine the headlines: 'Older man (distant relative of King David) makes teenage girl pregnant'. They'd not slept together, so Joseph knew without a shadow of a doubt that he wasn't the father. He wrongly assumed that Mary must have been cheating on him. His first reaction was to call the wedding off. That was until an angel visited him as well, and confirmed Mary's story that the baby was the Son of God. It was then that Joseph finally understood – and believed. He agreed to be the father of a child who was not naturally his, yet to love and raise him as if he was his own flesh and blood.

And that's the set of circumstances that led them to travel to Joseph's home town of Bethlehem while Mary was heavily pregnant and ready to give birth at any moment. The Romans had ordered that a census was to be taken – so everyone had to go to their own city to be counted. Their 80-mile journey would have been hard enough as it was, let alone for a heavily pregnant woman sitting on a donkey. Mary and Joseph's plan was probably to stay in Bethlehem for at least a year or two. As well as being part of the rules of the census, such a move would also have helped them to avoid the tittle-tattle of the village gossips back in Nazareth concerning a shotgun wedding.

Because of the census, Bethlehem was so crowded that all the hotels and pubs were full. 'No Vacancy' signs would have been hanging everywhere. The only place the expectant couple could stay was with the animals. So Jesus ended up coming into the world in a stable. The tiny new-born baby was wrapped in a blanket and laid in an animal feeding trough – the manger.

It's an unusual start when you sit back and really think about it. In many respects the means of Jesus' arrival on Planet Earth didn't make much sense at all. I mean, why did God choose a way of bringing his Son into the world that would bring so much controversy and misunderstanding? Why did he use an ordinary teenage girl, who wasn't even married, to give birth to the Son of God? Why let the legitimacy of his birth be doubted? Why were the very first witnesses to the birth a bunch of uneducated illiterate nobodies who smelt of sheep?

It's stupid to say, really, but of course God knew best. For, coming in this way, Jesus was human and divine, all in one. There was no other way that he could have been both. God could have sent him from heaven as a man, but he wouldn't have been human. He could have been born normally as we are, but then he wouldn't have been divine. The only way was to be born of an earthly mum so he was human, yet his real father was God, so he was also divine. This was no happy accident. It was all part of God's master plan.

Also, the other important point is that Jesus, while human, didn't sin. Remember the concept of 'original' or 'inherited' sin from the last chapter? To recap, it's the belief that all humans sin because they have inherited this sinful nature from the original father of us all, Adam. But, of course, Jesus didn't have an earthly father like us. He didn't need to sin.

A real person

As a baby Jesus would have learnt to eat, crawl, then eventually when he was probably one year old would have mastered the art of toddling. After a couple more years he went on to read and write. The Bible tells us he grew up quite normally as a child into an adult: 'And the child grew and became strong; he was filled with wisdom, and the grace of God was upon him' (Luke 2:40). Later on Luke tells us: 'And Jesus grew in wisdom and stature, and in favour with God and men' (Luke 2:52).

Jesus was perfectly normal. It's not too surprising to read that, after fasting for forty days in the wilderness, 'he was hungry' (Matthew 4:2). We also learn that on a long journey from Judea to Galilee he stopped off in Samaria: 'Jacob's well was there, and Jesus, tired as he was from the journey, sat down by the well. It was about the sixth hour. When a Samaritan woman came to draw water, Jesus said to her, "Will you give me a drink?" ' (John 4:6–7). So it's clear that he got tired and thirsty, too. We know Jesus worked as a carpenter for much of his life, so he must have been physically strong. He also spoke to large crowds of people without the benefit of a microphone and PA system, so he must have had a powerful voice. He was humorous and kind, but we also read of occasions when he lost his temper and was angry.

Dare I say it, but he also went to the toilet. I hope you don't think I'm being flippant, irreverent or simply labouring the point, but it's important for us to understand that Jesus was a flesh-and-blood human being, just like us. Jesus was no wimp in a white nightie and sandals, with a fluorescent halo floating above his head. Neither was he a figment of people's imaginations. Tacitus, a Roman historian in AD 112, writes about the reign of the Emperor Nero and refers to Jesus and the Christians in Rome (*Annals*, XV, 44). Soon after this, Pliny the Younger, once described as one of the world's great letter-writers, writes an interesting letter about Christianity to the Emperor Trajan. In it he mentions the early Christians singing hymns, worshipping Jesus as God, and pledging themselves not to do wicked things but instead to live moral lives. This is what he said:

> They were in the habit of meeting on a certain fixed day before it was light, when they sang in alternate verses a hymn to Christ, as to a god, and bound themselves by a solemn oath, not to do any wicked deeds, never to commit any fraud, theft or adultery, never to falsify their word, nor deny a trust when they should be called upon to deliver it up.

Bear in mind that these words come from a pagan writer. Jesus was a flesh-and-blood historical figure. In Jesus we have the most amazing man who ever lived, and yet it was the prostitutes, lepers and thieves who loved him, and the religious who hated his guts.

Totally sinless

Some intellectual graffiti was once found on a wall of St John's College, Cambridge: 'Jesus said unto them: "Who do you say that I am?" And they replied: "You are the eschatological manifestation of the ground of our being, the kerygma in which we find the ultimate meaning of our interpersonal relationships." And Jesus said: "What?" '

We've seen that Jesus was very real and very human, but the Bible does tell us that Jesus was also very different, for he never did, said or thought anything wrong. He was totally and utterly sinless. For example, we read in the New Testament how Satan threw everything at Jesus in the wilderness for forty days and nights. However, he was unable to tempt him in any shape or form whatsoever: 'When the devil had finished all this tempting, he left him until an opportune time' (Luke 4:13).

The author of Hebrews agrees that Jesus was tempted, yet never sinned: 'For we do not have a high priest who is unable to sympathise with our weaknesses, but we have one who has been tempted in every way, just as we are – yet was without sin' (Hebrews 4:15). The sinlessness of Jesus is taught throughout the New Testament. Paul referred to Jesus as: 'God made him who had no sin to be sin for us, so that in him we might become the righteousness of God' (2 Corinthians 5:21). Peter spoke of Jesus as: 'a lamb without blemish or defect' (1 Peter 1:19). He continued: 'For Christ died for sins once for all, the righteous for the unrighteous, to bring you to God' (1 Peter 3:18).

Words and actions

The American astronaut James Irwin, one of the few men to have experienced the sensation of walking on the moon, said, 'Jesus walking on the earth is far more important than man walking on the moon.' Let's take a brief look at Jesus' time on earth and examine just some of the things that he said and did that made him so special.

He said we are all important
He once told a story about a farmer with a hundred sheep who lost one of them. He left the ninety-nine to look for the lost sheep. He is happier about finding that one sheep than the ninety-nine that were never lost. In the same way God doesn't want any of us to be lost; he wants to find us and for us to find him, whoever and wherever we are.

Someone once said that if God had a wallet he would have your photo in it. He'd wander around heaven, proudly showing your picture to everyone he could find. It's a wonderful illustration that helps us realise God's love for each individual.

He said he was the only way to God

Jesus said, 'I am the way and the truth and the life. No one comes to the Father except through me' (John 14:6). It could sound like an incredibly arrogant statement unless it really is true. Jesus' statement kind of dismisses the old adage that 'all roads somehow lead to God'. Now certainly other religions have elements of truth and some great moral teaching, but look at those words of Jesus again: 'I am the way and the truth and the life.' Christianity is about people knowing God in a personal way through Jesus – the one and only way to God.

He healed people

Jesus' work began with teaching and healing. He didn't just talk about the power of God, he actually demonstrated it as well, and, not surprisingly, crowds from all over Palestine flocked to see him. One day in Capernaum, his disciple Peter told him about his mother-in-law who was suffering from a fever; Jesus touched her and the fever left immediately (Matthew 8:14–16).

Another day, as Jesus was healing people in a house, some men tried to bring in their paralysed friend to him. They couldn't get in because of the vast crowds so they went on to the roof and started to dig through the layers upon layers of clay, grass and branches to make a hole through which they could lower the man through the ceiling. Now that's what I call a pretty impressive entrance. Jesus saw them and, seeing their faith, healed him (Luke 5:17–26).

He also healed lepers, a deformed and withered hand, deafness and dumbness, blindness, a severed ear, bleeding and a disease called dropsy that caused the body to swell. The thing is, though, most of Jesus' miracles weren't even recorded, and the ones we know about are just some of the incredible things he did to show God's wonderful compassion and love for people.

He turned water into wine

Being an interesting sort of person, Jesus once got invited to a wedding and the party afterwards. He was there with his family and friends and then the organisers ran out of wine, a major problem! Unlike our short weddings today, with the service over in an hour and then a two-hour reception, in Jesus' day it was quite a bit more than mushroom vol-au-vents, sausage rolls and a slice of cake. Weddings then usually took about a week. On the first day, the bride and groom exchanged vows under a canopy, then for the next six days or more the happy couple and all the guests celebrated with dancing, games, music, food and wine. It sounds quite a party, doesn't it, and it was – until they ran out of wine. The Bible tells us Jesus went and found six jars of water, each holding around 100 litres, and he miraculously turned the contents into the finest vintage wine – certainly not plonk. We're talking well over nine hundred bottles' worth of Chateau Mouton Rothschild or Montrachet – or, rather, the first century's equivalent.

He raised the dead

On three different occasions Jesus brought people back from the dead. One day in a small town called Nain, some 10 miles south-east of Nazareth, Jesus stood and watched a funeral procession. It was a heartbreaking sight – a devastated widow, her husband already deceased and now her only son dead too. The coffin, not like our modern coffins, was probably just a board on which the body lay. The mourning cortège passed by and Jesus stopped it. He told the boy's mother to stop crying, and told the corpse to get up. The young man sat up immediately and began to talk.

He forgave sin

In the New Testament the Greek word most often used for 'forgiveness' actually means 'sending away' or 'release'. Literally, it's the taking away of wrong-doing and the guilt that goes with it. Jesus once told a story of a wayward son who rebelled against his father (Luke 15 – the Prodigal Son) but who was received back with open arms and forgiveness. I'm sure we all know from personal experience that forgiveness isn't always an easy thing, and in many ways it has a real cost to it. Christians believe that through Jesus' death and resurrection he made God's forgiveness possible for our wrong thoughts, words and actions. In other words, God's forgiveness cost God the life of his one and only Son.

He claimed to be God

In 1936, a radio broadcast was transmitted to America from England. Just before the voice of King Edward VIII was to be heard, someone tripped over a wire in the control room at the radio station and snapped the only line of communication between the two countries. The engineers were frantic. With only a few moments remaining before airtime a quick-thinking apprentice grasped the two broken ends of the wire and bridged the gap. Seconds later, the King addressed the nation. In a very real sense, his words were being transmitted through the body of that man.

That, of course, is the very essence of Christianity. Christians believe that Jesus was God in human form – that Jesus was God in a body. He didn't come to stop suffering, he came to suffer with us. He came to experience every emotion that we feel: laughter, hope, pain, despair. God entered our time–space world to experience it first-hand for himself and to make a difference.

These examples that I've mentioned are just scratching the surface, really. It's hardly any wonder that John wrote in his book, 'Jesus did many other things as well. If every one of them were written down, I suppose that even the whole world would not have room for the books that would be written' (John 21:25).

It's fascinating that, in total, only fifty or so days of Jesus' work are touched upon in the combined Gospel accounts. That's not a lot in three years of public travelling, or, put another way, a thousand days or so. That means less than 5 per cent of the days Jesus was ministering are actually recorded. Just imagine all the conversations, the fun and laughter, and indeed all the other miraculous things we've never even heard about.

Final days

Jesus had been travelling and preaching for around three years with his radical words and actions. We've looked briefly at just a handful of them. Understandably he had made many friends but many enemies too – mainly of the religious variety, and they schemed and plotted to kill him. He spoke out against religion and its endless rules and regulations, and talked about 'life' – indeed, abundant life, through knowing God. This new life was for everyone, Jew and Gentile. Jesus was a breath of fresh air and upset the status quo of old religion.

The time was April AD 30, and Jesus' extraordinary life was about to come to an end. While he was in Bethany, the Sanhedrin (the Jewish court) were meeting in the High Priest's palace to arrange for his arrest and execution. Jesus' work was almost over.

He knew his mission was nearing its end, and so he wanted to spend his last days with his best friends. He arranged a meal, which has become known as the Last Supper, where they sat and ate unleavened bread and drank red wine. Jesus knew that there was a traitor sitting around the table, and that one of his closest friends, one of his very own disciples, was about to betray him. It was now inevitable. After supper, they sang a hymn together and then went to a garden called Gethsemane, on the west slope of the Mount of Olives, to pray.

Gethsemane means 'oil press', and was probably originally an orchard of olive trees surrounded by a wall. It was here that Jesus agonised as he mentally prepared himself for what lay ahead.

While he was praying and talking to his friends, Judas his betrayer arrived with a crowd of temple police carrying swords and clubs. One of the disciples put up a bit of a fight, but soon realised that it was futile and so fled and left Jesus all alone. He was then led away to his accusers.

Accusations

Practically every legal rule was broken in an attempt to convict Jesus. Jewish law had banned trials at night, during the festival of Passover, and without witnesses – yet all of this happened during Jesus' trial. The whole case should have been dismissed; it was a total sham. He was taken initially to the High Priest's house. Joseph Caiaphas had been High Priest for eighteen years and was desperate to find something false against Jesus, particularly some evidence that the Roman governor would recognise. Many people came and told lies and gave false evidence but the Council could still find no reason to kill him.

Jesus endured three different religious trials and eventually the High Priest charged him with blasphemy, as he claimed to be equal to God. Then the people spat in his face and beat him up. Having orchestrated the arrest, trial and the false witnesses, the religious Chief Priests still had to ensure that the execution took place. For this they needed Roman authority, and this is why Jesus was taken to Pilate, very early the next morning.

Pontius Pilate was the Roman governor of Judea between AD 26 and 37. Cruel and unpopular with the Jews, he was afraid his unpopularity with them would mean the loss of his office. In the case of Jesus, he even tried to shirk the responsibility of a final decision by trying to get Herod, the governor of Galilee, who happened to be in Jerusalem at the time, to take over the case. Between them they had declared Jesus innocent of all the charges brought against him and desperately wanted to release him. He was innocent, but the crowds were not interested in justice, instead only in his death.

Passions and tempers were inflamed, and the Jews seemed ready to riot. Afraid that he would be accused before Caesar, Pilate, a very weak man, once again tried to extricate himself from the situation and remove all responsibility from himself for the final decision about to be made: he got the angry crowd to decide for him. They made their feelings crystal clear. So Pilate 'took water and washed his hands in front of the crowd. "I am innocent of this man's blood," he said. "It is your responsibility!" ' (Matthew 27:24). The death sentence had been passed.

Crucifixion

There's no doubt about it, crucifixion was the most painful public and bloody death in the first century. Once it had been decided to crucify a person, it was customary for the condemned man to be brutally beaten half to death. The Roman soldiers would have used a whip consisting of long leather strips bound together at one end into a strong handle. Into each of these strips would be sewn sharp pieces of bone and lead to inflict serious damage. Jesus would have been stripped naked and tied to a vertical post, and then the whip would be lashed against his shoulders, back and legs, the first lashes tearing into the skin, further lashes causing more serious damage.

Eusebius, a third-century historian, described the flogging of prisoners with graphic words: 'The sufferer's veins were laid bare, and the very muscles, sinews and bowels of the victim were opened to exposure.' The centurion in charge would have stopped the beating when he reckoned the prisoner was near death. It was also customary after the beating to mock the prisoner, and the Bible tells us this is what happened to Jesus. He was forced to wear a purple robe and a crown, made out of thorns, that was pushed on to his head. A jeering mob hurled more abuse and spat on him as he was led to the place where he was to be crucified, Golgotha, which means 'the place of the Skull'.

His back had been torn to shreds, yet he had to carry the wooden crossbeam on which he was to be crucified. He would have been marched through the streets by the longest route as a warning to everyone else not to mess with the Romans. On the way he collapsed and a man called Simon, who was from Tripoli in North Africa, was pulled out of the crowd to carry his cross. He would have been Jewish and had probably scraped and saved all his life to visit Jerusalem during the Passover, and now he'd got involved with carrying Jesus' cross. Behind them followed a group of women who were crying. Jesus turned around and told them not to cry for him. He knew that it was all part of God's plan.

When they arrived at the execution site, large nails were banged into his wrists and feet, and the cross was lifted up into position and jarred into the ground, racking the body with excruciating pain. First the religious rulers, then the Roman soldiers shouted and threw insults at him. But even then Jesus said, 'Father, forgive them, because they don't know what they're doing.' Death was now only a matter of time.

Crucifixion was a brutal way to kill someone. The Roman statesman, lawyer and scholar, Cicero, called it 'the most cruel and hideous of tortures' – and it certainly was. What actually used to kill people, apart from the pain, blood loss, shock and trauma, was asphyxia or, as it is more commonly known, suffocation. The human body, hanging from the arms, had to keep pushing itself up just to breathe – and remember, nails were through the feet. In the end the pain got just too much and the prisoner suffocated. Incidentally, if the person was taking too long to die, the guards would break both legs, making it impossible to push up. After that, death was very quick indeed. This wasn't necessary in Jesus' case as he was already dead when the guards came.

Death

Just before he died, he shouted, 'It is finished' (John 19:30). When we look at the phrase translated back into the original Greek it becomes *tetelestai*. Archaeologists have repeatedly found its Latin equivalent, *consummatum est*, scrawled against ancient tax receipts, indicating that they had been 'paid in full'. Christians believe Jesus' death made it possible for us to know forgiveness for the wrong that we do, and that Jesus paid the price for the sin that separates us from God – he wiped the slate clean.

The moment he died the sun went dark and a curtain was torn in the Temple. The darkening sky was a supernatural occurrence and was a sign to the Romans and the other non-Jews. The tearing of the curtain had a great deal of religious significance for the Jews, as the curtain represented separation between God and man, and now it was destroyed. Access to God was made available through Jesus and was now the right of anyone, Jew and non-Jew alike.

Anyway, back to the dead body. Don't forget it was imperative that Jesus was dead, as he had openly said that he would come back to life. To make sure, one of his executioners thrust a spear into his side and blood and water came out. Blood came from the heart, and doctors have told us that the watery fluid came from the sac surrounding the heart, and therefore Jesus probably died not from suffocation but of massive heart failure. Quite literally, he died from a broken heart.

The dead body was dealt with in accordance with Jewish burial traditions. Jesus' body would have been removed from the cross and covered with a sheet, then immediately taken to a private tomb owned by a wealthy supporter. The Jews considered the washing of the body very important, so this would have been done once they were inside the tomb, and then the body was covered in spices and a white linen cloth. Everyone then left the tomb and a large stone was rolled into place across the front.

Modern engineers have reckoned that this stone, a huge disc-shaped boulder, would have weighed between 1.5 and 2 tonnes, and would have taken perhaps twenty men to move it once it was in position in a groove or trench to the front of the tomb. Even Clark Kent's alter ego, Superman, would have raised quite a sweat moving it once gravity had done its job and it was in place in its groove.

While all this was going on, the Jewish authorities were in a state of panic, because even though Jesus was finally dead thousands were becoming Christians. To avoid any doubt over his death, a well-trained Roman guard was sent to secure the tomb where the body lay. If this hundred-man unit wasn't enough security, a seal was set on the stone to prevent anyone from tampering with the tomb in which his body lay. This seal was in fact a cord that was stretched across the massive stone in front of the tomb and fastened at each end with clay. Finally, the clay was imprinted with the official signet of the Roman governor of the time. Tampering with this official seal held serious consequences, and anyone breaking it would have incurred the full force of the Roman law. The guards were on full alert and the tomb secured. The dead body was going nowhere.

A great victory

Even though it might not have seemed like it at the time, and certainly not to his disciples, who ran away and hid for fear of their lives, Jesus had won the greatest victory of all time. His barbaric death achieved many incredible things.

First, he died in our place. We read that 'Then Christ would have had to suffer many times since the creation of the world. But now he has appeared once for all at the end of the ages to do away with sin by the sacrifice of himself' (Hebrews 9:26). He gave himself so that we could know God for ourselves. He sacrificed his own life so that we might have life.

Jesus also became a way through which we could become reconciled to God. Remember how our sin has separated us from God ever since the fall of mankind in Eden? 'All this is from God, who reconciled us to himself through Christ and gave us the ministry of reconciliation: that God was reconciling the world to himself in Christ, not counting men's sins against them. And he has committed to us the message of reconciliation' (2 Corinthians 5:18–19). It's as though Jesus bridged the gap between us and God.

Third, because we are all sinners, we are in bondage and held captive to sin. We're programmed to sin, we just can't help doing it. We often read of prisoners kidnapped and held captive until a ransom is paid – well, that's another image that Jesus gave us as he prophesied his death:'For even the Son of Man did not come to be served, but to serve, and to give his life as a ransom for many' (Mark 10:45). Because Jesus paid the ransom with his own life, we are now set free – if we want.

Delving deeper

Why did Jesus come?
1 Luke 19:10
2 John 3:16–17
3 John 10:9
4 1 Timothy 1:15
5 Hebrews 2:14–15

How did he take the punishment our sins deserve?
1 Matthew 27:46
2 Romans 5:8
3 Galatians 3:13
4 2 Corinthians 5:21
5 Colossians 1:19–20

What other names was Jesus known by?

1. Matthew 1:23
2. Matthew 16:16
3. Luke 22:22
4. John 1:14
5. John 1:29
6. John 10:11
7. John 14:6
8. John 15:1
9. Galatians 2:20
10. 1 Timothy 4:10

Memory verse

The Word became flesh and made his dwelling among us. We have seen his glory, the glory of the One and Only, who came from the Father, full of grace and truth.

(John 1:14)

4

Resurrection and Ascension

> Christianity is in its very essence a resurrection religion.
> The concept of resurrection lies at its heart. If you remove
> it, Christianity is destroyed.
>
> *John R.W. Stott*

Some years ago, Frank Morrison, an English journalist, started
to write a book to show that the resurrection never happened.
After considerable research he realised that the resurrection really
did happen, and he became a Christian. This is what Morrison
said in the introduction to his book, *Who Moved the Stone?*

> This study is in some ways so unusual and provocative that
> the writer thinks it desirable to state here very briefly how
> the book came to take its present form. In one sense it
> could have taken no other, for it is essentially a confession,
> the inner story of a man who originally set out to write
> one kind of book and found himself compelled by the
> sheer force of circumstances to write another.

We're about to look at a short passage that pretty much sums up
what we've looked at so far in this book. The words come from

Romans, a book that the Apostle Paul wrote to the Christians in Rome around AD 56. Paul had been faithfully preaching the gospel since his conversion some twenty years earlier, during which time he had founded churches throughout the Mediterranean world. He writes this book as he is nearing the end of his third missionary journey, and it is therefore an important and profound statement of his understanding of the Christian message:

> Therefore, since we have been justified through faith, we have peace with God through our Lord Jesus Christ, through whom we have gained access by faith into this grace in which we now stand. And we rejoice in the hope of the glory of God. Not only so, but we also rejoice in our sufferings, because we know that suffering produces perseverance; perseverance, character; and character, hope. And hope does not disappoint us, because God has poured out his love into our hearts by the Holy Spirit, whom he has given us.
>
> You see, at just the right time, when we were still powerless, Christ died for the ungodly. Very rarely will anyone die for a righteous man, though for a good man someone might possibly dare to die. But God demonstrates his own love for us in this: While we were still sinners, Christ died for us.
>
> Since we have now been justified by his blood, how much more shall we be saved from God's wrath through him!
>
> (Romans 5:1–9)

That word 'access' at the start of the passage actually means 'introduction'. Jesus has introduced us to God through his life, death and resurrection. He made it possible for us to live in friendship with God. Jesus' dying was the only way God could save men, women, boys and girls. There was no other way.

During the American Civil War, a farmer was called up to fight in the war. He was deeply concerned about leaving his family. His wife had died some years earlier and there would be no one to support and take care of his children while he was away. The day before he was to leave for the army, his neighbour came to visit him. He said to the astonished farmer, 'I've been thinking. You're needed here at home, so I've decided to go in your place.' The farmer was so overwhelmed that for a few moments he was speechless. The offer seemed too good to be true. He grasped the hand of the young man and praised God for this friend who was willing to go in his place as his substitute. The young man went to the front lines and fought bravely, but his short life was ended when he was shot and killed in the first battle.

When the farmer heard the news, he immediately saddled his horse and rode out to the battlefield. After searching for some time, he found the body of his friend. He arranged to have it buried in the churchyard near the spot where the two of them had often stopped to talk after the services. On a piece of marble that was to be the headstone of the grave, he carved an inscription with his own hands. It was roughly done, but with every blow of the hammer on the chisel tears fell from his eyes. Many villagers wept as they read the brief but touching inscription: 'HE DIED FOR ME'.

When Jesus died on a Roman cross he died for you and me. His death made it possible for us to be set free from sin. It's as if he took our place and the punishment our sin deserves: 'But God demonstrates his own love for us in this: While we were still sinners, Christ died for us' (Romans 5:8). As we've already seen, through the cross Jesus made it possible for us to know forgiveness and to know God.

Let me recap for just a moment on the chain of events surrounding his death. On the very first Good Friday in April AD 30, Jesus was executed. He was dead, there was no doubt about it. He had been brutally beaten, then crucified. To make sure he was dead a Roman soldier stuck his spear into his side. The Bible tells us that blood and water poured out, from his heart. His body was taken down from the cross and placed in a tomb, and the grave was then guarded.

Resurrection

On that first Easter Sunday, the women who approached the tomb couldn't fail to notice that the massive stone covering the tomb had been moved and that the soldiers had fled, an offence so grave it would normally have resulted in the death penalty for these 'deserters'. None of them were punished, though, on this occasion – indeed, it looks as if they were 'paid off' by the authorities to keep their silence. This was quite extraordinary.

The women paused, puzzled by the whole scene, when suddenly two men in bright shining clothes stood before them. Absolutely terrified, the women fell to the ground as the men told them that Jesus had been raised from the dead. As they were leaving, one of the women, Mary Magdalene, then saw Jesus for herself. It was probably quite dark and initially she didn't properly recognise him; instead, she assumed it was the caretaker, doing a few odd jobs around the cemetery.

If the whole thing had been some elaborate hoax or scam that had been planned by his friends and disciples, then they had been incredibly stupid in making the women the first witnesses on the scene. I know it sounds incredibly sexist, but in those days the testimony of women was not valid in a court of law. A small, but I believe not insignificant, point.

Later that same day Jesus suddenly appeared to the disciples. He was alive, just as he'd promised. They'd returned to their old jobs as fishermen and saw him while they were out on a fishing expedition. Not surprisingly, they were pretty startled and frightened and they thought they were seeing a ghost. Take a look at just one of the Gospel accounts:

When they landed, they saw a fire of burning coals there with fish on it, and some bread. Jesus said to them, 'Bring some of the fish you have just caught.' Simon Peter climbed aboard and dragged the net ashore. It was full of large fish, 153, but even with so many the net was not torn. Jesus said to them, 'Come and have breakfast.' None of the disciples dared ask him, 'Who are you?' They knew it was the Lord. Jesus came, took the bread and gave it to them, and did the same with the fish.

(John 21:9–13)

Jesus later organised a beach barbecue where he cooked breakfast for them. He let the disciples touch him and he actually ate grilled fish in front of them to prove he wasn't some sort of ghostly apparition.

This was just the start, though. For over a month he appeared again to his disciples and others on eleven different occasions. Indeed, at one time he was seen by more than five hundred people in one go. This was not mass hysteria, or a hallucination or wishful thinking. Jesus was most definitely alive. It was all true, and it is a crucial part of our faith. Paul actually said we're all wasting our time if it isn't true: 'And if Christ has not been raised, our preaching is useless and so is your faith' (1 Corinthians 15:14). Christianity is a religion of the empty tomb. The resurrection was essential. It proved that Jesus wasn't just a good man. He was the God man.

Ascension

After forty days it was finally time for Jesus to leave. He'd explained to his disciples that he had to go but wouldn't leave them completely alone, as he would send the Holy Spirit to give them power for their lives: 'But I tell you the truth: It is for your good that I am going away. Unless I go away, the Counsellor will not come to you; but if I go, I will send him to you' (John

16:7–8). Unlike God, Jesus could only be in one place at a time. Through the Holy Spirit Jesus could be available to the whole world.

So his time on earth was over. He had lived, died, risen from the dead, people had touched him and he had eaten with them, and now he was going back to be with his father. He made a final and miraculous departure as he ascended into heaven. Luke gives an account of the ascension not just once, but twice: 'When he had led them out to the vicinity of Bethany, he lifted up his hands and blessed them. While he was blessing them, he left them and was taken up into heaven' (Luke 24:50–1).

Then in the book of Acts Luke gives us his second report of what happened on that day:

> He was taken up before their very eyes, and a cloud hid him from their sight.
>
> They were looking intently up into the sky as he was going, when suddenly two men dressed in white stood beside them. 'Men of Galilee,' they said, 'why do you stand here looking into the sky? This same Jesus, who has been taken from you into heaven, will come back in the same way you have seen him go into heaven.'
>
> (Acts 1:9–11)

The ascension was a remarkable conclusion to Jesus' time on earth. It was important that Jesus didn't simply wander off and spend the rest of his life on earth in retirement and obscurity. Also, he didn't just disappear from sight never to be seen again. He very deliberately went up to heaven. The disciples actually saw with their own eyes Jesus gradually ascending up in the sky and finally disappearing from sight as he passed through the clouds. Jesus was going to a place, and this place was called heaven.

He had completed his mission on earth. Jesus had lived an incredible life and through his death and resurrection had paid the penalty for our sins. The writer of Hebrews tells us that now in heaven Jesus would sit at the right hand of God: 'The Son is the radiance of God's glory and the exact representation of his being, sustaining all things by his powerful word. After he had provided purification for sins, he sat down at the right hand of the Majesty in heaven' (Hebrews 1:3).

That's a lovely picture. When you or I have completed a job, or done a hard day's graft, there's nothing better than sitting down in your favourite chair with a cup of tea or a can of beer. It works for me every time. I hope you don't think I'm being irreverent here, as I do believe that that's the scene the writer of Hebrews describes about Jesus – minus the tea and beer, of course. His job on earth was finished. It went just to plan, so he sat down. Done and dusted. Mission accomplished.

By this point you may be wondering if the ascension has anything to do with you. The answer's simple: yes, it does. Before he left for heaven, Jesus assured all believers that they would go there too:

> In my Father's house are many rooms; if it were not so, I would have told you. I am going there to prepare a place for you. And if I go and prepare a place for you, I will come back and take you to be with me that you also may be where I am. You know the way to the place where I am going.
>
> (John 14:2–4)

This 'place' was heaven, and one day we'll go there too to live with him for ever. It's going to be fantastic.

Delving deeper

Did Jesus actually rise from the dead?
1 Matthew 28:6
2 Mark 16:9
3 Luke 24:15
4 John 20:19–23
5 John 20:24–30

What did Jesus achieve when he rose from the dead?
1 Acts 17:31
2 Romans 1:4
3 Romans 4:25
4 Romans 6:9
5 1 Peter 1:3

Where did Jesus go when he left earth?
1 Luke 24:50–1
2 Acts 1:9–11
3 Acts 2:33
4 1 Timothy 3:16
5 Hebrews 1:4

Memory verse

And if Christ has not been raised, our preaching is useless and so is your faith.

(1 Corinthians 15:14)

5

Repentance and Faith

God creates out of nothing. Therefore until a man is nothing, God can make nothing out of him.

Martin Luther

Gary Inrig, in his book *Hearts of Iron, Feet of Clay*, told of a well-known evangelist whom God used in a significant way in Britain some years ago. The evangelist turned his back on God and drifted into a life of sin for a number of months. For a while he managed to keep it all secret, but ultimately the truth came out and because of the man's profile the sensational news even made the newspaper headlines. At first, all he could think of was that he had been ruined for life, but finally he realised what an idiot he had been and he came back to God like the prodigal son (see Luke 15:11–32).

He found exactly the same thing the prodigal did. God welcomed him with open arms and began to strengthen him and forgive him. Finally, after a period of waiting, he felt he should start preaching the gospel again. In the back of his mind he was always afraid that his sin would be brought up all over again, but after he felt sure it was completely dealt with and a thing of the past, he went back to preaching, knowing that God had forgiven him completely.

One night, when he arrived in Aberdeen, he was given a sealed letter. Just before the service began, he read the unsigned letter. It described the shameful series of events he had been previously involved in. As far as he was concerned his sin had been dealt with by God – not just forgiven, but completely forgotten as well. Now this anonymous author wanted to bring it all back up again. His stomach churned as he read. The letter said, 'If you have the nerve to preach tonight, I'll stand up and expose you again.'

He read the letter again and immediately fell to his knees in prayer. A few minutes later, he was preaching in the pulpit. He began his talk by reading the letter, from start to finish. Then he said, 'I want to make it clear that this letter is perfectly true. I'm ashamed of what I've read, and what I've done. I come tonight, not as one who is perfect, but as one who is forgiven.' God used that letter and the rest of his ministry as a magnet to draw many people to Jesus.

Knowing isn't enough

In the Millennium Poll conducted by MORI for the *Sunday Telegraph* in December 1999, adults in Great Britain were asked, among other things, about faith and religion. The survey said that 71 per cent of Britons believed in God. That's a lot of people, really, when you think about it. But as you've seen by getting this far in the book, belief in God doesn't automatically make someone a Christian. Knowing about God or even accepting that Jesus was the Son of God isn't enough. In the Bible, an intelligent man called Nicodemus knew a great deal about Jesus. He believed that God had sent him, but as we see from his encounter with Jesus in the dead of night, he had lots to learn:

Now there was a man of the Pharisees named Nicodemus, a member of the Jewish ruling council. He came to Jesus at night and said, 'Rabbi, we know you are a teacher who has come from God. For no one could perform the miraculous signs you are doing if God were not with him.'

In reply Jesus declared, 'I tell you the truth, no one can see the kingdom of God unless he is born again.'

'How can a man be born when he is old?' Nicodemus asked. 'Surely he cannot enter a second time into his mother's womb to be born!'

Jesus answered, 'I tell you the truth, no one can enter the kingdom of God unless he is born of water and the Spirit. Flesh gives birth to flesh, but the Spirit gives birth to spirit. You should not be surprised at my saying, "You must be born again." The wind blows wherever it pleases. You hear its sound, but you cannot tell where it comes from or where it is going. So it is with everyone born of the Spirit.'

'How can this be?' Nicodemus asked.

'You are Israel's teacher,' said Jesus, 'and do you not understand these things? I tell you the truth, we speak of what we know, and we testify to what we have seen, but still you people do not accept our testimony. I have spoken to you of earthly things and you do not believe; how then will you believe if I speak of heavenly things? No one has ever gone into heaven except the one who came from heaven – the Son of Man. Just as Moses lifted up the snake in the desert, so the Son of Man must be lifted up, that everyone who believes in him may have eternal life.

'For God so loved the world that he gave his one and only Son, that whoever believes in him shall not perish but have eternal life. For God did not send his Son into the world to condemn the world, but to save the world through him. Whoever believes in him is not condemned, but whoever does not believe stands condemned already because he has not believed in the name of God's one and only Son.'

(John 3:1–18)

We can see from the story that Nicodemus was an important man. He was a religious leader and a member of the Sanhedrin, the Jewish ruling council. He was a big cheese. Maybe that's why he came in the middle of the night so that there was no way he would be spotted by one of his fellow Pharisees. During his late-night chat he finally began to realise that knowing about Jesus was not enough. Eventually the penny dropped. He needed to believe in him.

For people today it's exactly the same. If going to church makes you a Christian then it's like saying that going to McDonald's makes you a hamburger. Reading the Bible is great. So is being nice to people, giving money to charity or helping little old ladies across the road – even if they don't want to go! But it's not enough. There's much more to it, and repentance and faith in Jesus are key.

Hearing and doing

Repentance is a deep sorrow for what has been done in the past and a turning away from all you know to be wrong. It's a case of not just *saying* sorry, but *being* sorry as well. Indeed, true repentance is to stop sinning, full stop.

The author C.S. Lewis described it like this:

Fallen man is not simply an imperfect creature who needs improvement; he is a rebel who must lay down his arms. This process of surrender, this movement full speed astern, is what Christians call repentance. Now repentance is no fun at all. It is something much harder than merely eating humble pie. It means unlearning all the self-conceit and self-will that we have been training ourselves into for thousands of years. It means killing part of yourself, under-going a kind of death.

Repentance is vital.

God commands it: 'now he commands all people everywhere to repent. For he has set a day when he will judge the world with justice by the man he has appointed. He has given proof of this to all men by raising him from the dead' (Acts 17:30–1).

Jesus urged the crowds to do it, to avoid destruction: 'But unless you repent, you too will all perish. Or those eighteen who died when the tower in Siloam fell on them – do you think they were more guilty than all the others living in Jerusalem? I tell you, no! But unless you repent, you too will all perish' (Luke 13:3–5).

Some years later, the Apostle Peter was preaching the gospel in Jerusalem. Those who heard his message were deeply convicted about their sin and rejection of Jesus and asked how they might be saved:

> When the people heard this, they were cut to the heart and said to Peter and the other apostles, 'Brothers, what shall we do?'
>
> Peter replied, 'Repent and be baptised, every one of you, in the name of Jesus Christ for the forgiveness of your sins. And you will receive the gift of the Holy Spirit. The promise is for you and your children and for all who are far off – for all whom the Lord our God will call.'
>
> (Acts 2:37–9)

The American author Bruce Larson once told the true story of a Catholic priest living in the Philippines, a much-loved man of God who carried throughout his life a guilty secret. He had committed a sin once, many years before, during his time in seminary. No one else knew of it, but it was hidden deep inside his heart and he could never forget it. He had repented of it and he had suffered years of remorse for it, but he still had no peace, no inner joy, no sense of God's forgiveness.

There was a woman in this priest's parish who deeply loved God, and who claimed to have visions in which she spoke with God and he with her. The priest, however, was rather sceptical of her claims, so to test her visions he said to her, 'You say you actually speak directly with God in your visions. Let me ask you a favour. The next time you have one of these visions, I want you to ask him what sin your priest committed while he was in seminary.'

The woman agreed and went home. When she returned to the church a few days later, the priest said, 'Well, did God visit you in your dreams?'

She replied, 'Yes, he did.'

'And did you ask him what sin I committed in seminary?'

'Yes, I asked him.'

'Well, what did he say?'

'He said, "I don't remember." '

This is what God wants us to know about the forgiveness he freely offers us when we truly repent. When our sins are forgiven, they are forgotten. The past – with its sins, hurts and brokenness – is gone, dead, crucified, remembered no more. What God forgives, he forgets.

Becoming a Christian

The story is told of a famous rabbi who was walking with some of his disciples when one of them asked, 'Rabbi, when should a man repent?'

The rabbi calmly replied, 'You should be sure you repent on the last day of your life.'

'But,' protested several of his disciples, 'we can never be sure which day will be the last day of our life.'

The famous rabbi smiled and said, 'The answer to that problem is very simple. Repent now.'

Both Peter and Paul talked about 'being saved'. You'll hear Christians talk about being 'born again', 'seeing the light', making a 'commitment to Christ', but basically they all mean the same thing. I personally like the term 'being saved' because to me it sums up the fact that before we knew Jesus we were lost, and now we're found because he's saved us.

Have a look at this wonderful piece of Scripture:

> As for you, you were dead in your transgressions and sins, in which you used to live when you followed the ways of this world and of the ruler of the kingdom of the air, the spirit who is now at work in those who are disobedient. All of us also lived among them at one time, gratifying the cravings of our sinful nature and following its desires and thoughts. Like the rest, we were by nature objects of wrath. But because of his great love for us, God, who is rich in mercy, made us alive with Christ even when we were dead in transgressions – it is by grace you have been saved.
>
> (Ephesians 2:1–5)

There's nothing we can do ourselves to become saved. We need the help of a Saviour.

Jesus – the only way

Jesus is the only way, and he offers an open invitation to everyone: 'Come to me, all you who are weary and burdened, and I will give you rest. Take my yoke upon you and learn from me, for I am gentle and humble in heart, and you will find rest for your souls' (Matthew 11:28–9).

Paul explained his mission statement: 'I have declared to both Jews and Greeks that they must turn to God in repentance and have faith in our Lord Jesus' (Acts 20:21). The Bible makes it clear what we need to do to be 'saved'.

1 Repent – 2 Peter 3:9
2 Have faith in God – Mark 1:15
3 Turn to God – Acts 3:19
4 Be baptised – Acts 2:38

We've seen that true repentance is more than just saying sorry. It's a complete U-turn, a full 180 degrees. Jesus once had an encounter with a dodgy tax collector called Zacchaeus. He was a bit of a crook and despised by everyone who knew him. After his meeting with Jesus – actually, a meal at his house – his life was never the same again. One of his first actions was to put things right with those he had cheated:

> Zacchaeus stood up and said to the Lord, 'Look, Lord! Here and now I give half of my possessions to the poor, and if I have cheated anybody out of anything, I will pay back four times the amount.'
> Jesus said to him, 'Today salvation has come to this house, because this man, too, is a son of Abraham. For the Son of Man came to seek and to save what was lost.'
>
> (Luke 19:8–9)

For Zacchaeus those steps were very practical, but they must have had amazing implications for all who knew him. Part of repentance is putting things right with others you may have hurt through wrong actions on your part. My friend and fellow evangelist, J. John, was recently swamped with cash and stolen goods after giving a talk based on one of the Ten Commandments. During his sermon, 'How to Prosper with a Clear Conscience', more than ninety people put wallets, watches, CDs, coats, hotel towels, jewellery and £1,500 in cash into honesty bins. One of the more intriguing items was a valuable piece of diamond jewellery, left with a note from a woman saying that her mother had lost it and claimed it on her insurance, but had never told the insurance company she had found it again.

Some very clear and dramatic repentance was happening at those meetings. Why not put the book down for five minutes and consider some down-to-earth and practical steps that you may need to take to show others that you have truly changed? You may need to get rid of certain physical things, or maybe you need another Christian to pray with you over certain issues. I've discovered in my own Christian life that the confession of sins to another person as well as to God is very powerful and releasing. This is particularly helpful for those who have dabbled in the occult. I do believe that past involvement in seances, ouija boards, tarot cards, witchcraft, Eastern religions and other occult practices needs to be seriously addressed, so God can set you totally free.

Real faith

Many people have heard of the outstanding exploits of Blondin, the fearless tightrope walker. Blondin amused and amazed thousands of people as he made his way over Niagara Falls on a slender rope stretched from shore to shore. He never faltered or failed. But Blondin had a secret. As he made his way over the rope, he would keep his eyes fixed on a large silver star which he had fixed at the far end. The star was the centre of his attention and guided him to the other side.

As we live our lives as Christians we need to look to a star – the bright and morning star, Jesus. He has run the race and now asks us, his followers, to run the race, keeping our eyes fixed on himself as the goal:

> Therefore, since we are surrounded by such a great cloud
> of witnesses, let us throw off everything that hinders and
> the sin that so easily entangles, and let us run with persever-

ance the race marked out for us. Let us fix our eyes on Jesus, the author and perfector of our faith, who for the joy set before him endured the cross, scorning its shame, and sat down at the right hand of the throne of God.

(Hebrews 12:1–2)

As we've already seen, true faith is much more than just believing that God exists. I believe that the Prime Minister exists, but I don't actually know him personally. He doesn't call me up for a chat or ask me to give my opinion at Cabinet meetings, and I certainly don't get invited to soirees at 10 Downing Street. Faith in God is shown not just by what we believe, but by what we do. If I tell my four children that there are 300 billion stars in the universe, they'll believe me. But if I tell them a door has just been painted, they all have to touch it just to be sure!

Faith is a wonderful gift from God: 'For it is by grace you have been saved, through faith – and this not from yourselves, it is the gift of God' (Ephesians 2:8). There's lots of things you can do with a gift. You can hide it in the loft or put it away in the garage, or you can pass it on to someone else. You might choose to take it back to the shop and change it for something else. You might even try to pay for it, if it's something really special. The best thing to do with a gift is to say thanks and accept it. To say it again, there's nothing we can do to earn God's forgiveness: it's a gift – so receive it!

Keep going

Although we've been looking at repentance and faith as essential requisites to becoming a Christian, it doesn't stop when we've prayed the prayer. Repentance and faith continue throughout our Christian lives because, let's face it, we all mess up from time to time. We all think, say and do things that hurt ourselves, hurt others and hurt God.

Jesus encouraged his disciples in their daily prayers to 'Forgive us our debts, as we also have forgiven our debtors' (Matthew 6:12). The word 'debts' is a Jewish way of regarding sins. I certainly remember reciting the Lord's Prayer, from which this verse is taken, at school, and we used the word 'trespasses' instead of 'debts'. Whichever way you look at it, it's clear that Jesus is instructing his disciples to regularly say sorry and be sorry for their wrong-doing, and that, of course, applies to us, his disciples today.

As for faith – well, we need that throughout our lives. Some Christians are so afraid of failure that they become reserved, over-cautious and totally uninvolved in real life. They never seem to risk anything and consequently never seem to achieve anything for themselves or for God. Their motto is: 'To avoid the chance of failure, don't try anything.' On the other hand, those who are willing to make mistakes and risk failure are the ones who ultimately achieve great things. Instead of being filled with fear, they go forward in faith. Problems are challenges. While the problems may not all be solved, these people would rather live with that reality than have a clean sheet of no failures and no accomplishments. Former American president Benjamin Franklin said one time, 'The man who does things makes many mistakes, but he never makes the biggest mistake of all – doing nothing.'

Paul, who was a man of great faith following a dramatic conversion to Christianity, explained that it was what kept him going through thick and thin: 'I have been crucified with Christ and I no longer live, but Christ lives in me. The life I live in the body, I live by faith in the Son of God, who loved me and gave himself for me' (Galatians 2:20). The Christian life is never an easy option, but I can assure you it's the best way to live your life.

Before you 'delve deeper', let me ask you a question. Have you genuinely repented of all you know to be wrong and put your faith in God? If you haven't or if you're not sure, then this is the moment to make sure, so you know without a shadow of a doubt that you are truly 'saved'. Pray the following prayer, in your own head or out loud, but meaning every word from deep within your heart: God promises to hear your words.

Father God,
I am so sorry for my sins.
For all those things I've ever said, thought and done that are wrong, I'm truly sorry.
I choose to turn from these wrong things and walk in the opposite direction.
I believe that Jesus came to set me free from sin so that I could know you.
So forgive me from my sin,
And help me live for you for ever.
Amen.

Delving deeper

How important is repentance?
1 Matthew 4:17
2 Luke 2:38
3 Luke 5:32
4 Luke 13:3–5
5 Luke 24:47
6 Acts 2:38
7 Acts 3:19
8 Acts 17:30
9 2 Peter 3:9
10 1 John 1:9

What does repentance involve?
1 Mark 1:15
2 Luke 19:8
3 Acts 2:38
4 Acts 3:19

How do we get faith?
1 Acts 4:4
2 Acts 8:12
3 Romans 10:17
4 Ephesians 2:8

Memory verses

For God so loved the world that he gave his one and only Son, that whoever believes in him shall not perish but have eternal life. For God did not send his Son into the world to condemn the world, but to save the world through him.

(John 3:16–17)

6

Holy Spirit

Before we can be filled with the Spirit, the desire to be filled must be all-consuming. It must be for the time the biggest thing in the life, so acute, so intrusive as to crowd out everything else. The degree of fullness in any life accords perfectly with the intensity of true desire. We have as much of God as we actually want.

A.W. Tozer

New cars are produced every year but the three-wheeled Revette, launched in America back in 1974, certainly seemed well ahead of its time. Its space-age design and revolutionary new engine promised remarkable fuel consumption and attracted much attention.

The car's inventors persuaded many people to invest in the company to enable it to start production. But when the car appeared for its first public demonstration the engine ran for only a second or two and then refused to restart. Without power it was impossible to drive the ill-fated car. The display was an absolute disaster and all the investors pulled out.

If you're anything like me, you'll have probably owned a car or two like that. Without stretching the analogy too far, I guess you could say the same thing about our Christian lives. Without the power to live for Jesus things can go wrong. But the good news is that God's not left us alone to struggle through our lives striving to live for him, and that's where the Holy Spirit comes in – he gives us the power to live as a Christian.

After the resurrection and just before Jesus ascended into heaven, he made a wonderful promise to his friends and followers: 'I have much more to say to you, more than you can now bear. But when he, the Spirit of truth, comes, he will guide you into all truth' (John 16:13). Jesus didn't want to leave his followers all alone so he promised the Holy Spirit would be there to help them.

Pentecost

Ten days after Jesus had ascended into heaven the Holy Spirit came, during a religious festival called Pentecost. Held around the beginning of June, Pentecost actually means 'the fiftieth' and another name for the festival was 'the feast of weeks'. Held fifty days after Passover, it was a great and wonderful annual celebration to thank God for the crops. It was a public holiday for everyone, so Jerusalem would have been heaving with vast crowds from many different nations, and it's into this situation that all heaven broke out when the Holy Spirit came in power:

> When the day of Pentecost came, they were all together in one place. Suddenly a sound like the blowing of a violent wind came from heaven and filled the whole house where they were sitting. They saw what seemed to be tongues of fire that separated and came to rest on each of them. All of them were filled with the Holy Spirit and began to speak in other tongues as the Spirit enabled them.
>
> (Acts 2:1–4)

In his account, Luke describes how the Holy Spirit was released to the 120 Christians who were meeting in what is described as an 'upper room'. The Holy Spirit came upon them like a violent tornado tearing through their meeting, with flames landing on their heads, and they then all spontaneously started speaking in different languages. The first disciples, now called 'apostles', and their fellow believers received the Holy Spirit and they were never the same again. Frightened followers of Jesus became fearless ones as they received power from God. They were compelled to tell everyone they could about Jesus and the gospel, and it's no exaggeration to say that within just twenty years they had taken the good news to every corner of the Roman Empire, and beyond.

The Holy Spirit

As with our previous chapters, it's always helpful to go right back to basics and attempt to find a definition. Though as we've already seen, precise definitions aren't always easy, and the Holy Spirit is no exception.

The Holy Spirit is God

Then Peter said, 'Ananias, how is it that Satan has so filled your heart that you have lied to the Holy Spirit and have kept for yourself some of the money you received for the land? Didn't it belong to you before it was sold? And after it was sold, wasn't the money at your disposal? What made you think of doing such a thing? You have not lied to men but to God.'

(Acts 5:3–4)

A Christian couple, Ananias and Sapphira, were lying to God and their fellow Christians. The point that Luke is making here is that lying to the Holy Spirit is regarded as lying to God.

The Holy Spirit is a person

The Holy Spirit is definitely not an impersonal 'it'. I would never dream of calling one of my children an 'it'. They are each a little person, and in my case they are a 'he' and three 'she's'. It's exactly the same with the Holy Spirit, who is also often referred to as a 'counsellor' or 'comforter'. Try getting an 'it' to come around and give you help or advice. You'll not get very far. A person will help you, though. Here's just one example: 'When the Counsellor comes, whom I will send to you from the Father, the Spirit of truth who goes out from the Father, he will testify about me' (John 15:26).

The Holy Spirit equips us

I'm convinced that it's not a case of us using the Holy Spirit. Instead, it's the Holy Spirit who uses us. That's a big difference. The Holy Spirit helps us live for Jesus in many different ways:

Understanding the Bible

'But the Counsellor, the Holy Spirit, whom the Father will send in my name, will teach you all things and will remind you of everything I have said to you' (John 14:26). The Holy Spirit will help us understand what we read in God's word, the Bible.

Sharing our faith with others

'When the Counsellor comes, whom I will send to you from the Father, the Spirit of truth who goes out from the Father, he will testify about me. And you also must testify, for you have been with me from the beginning' (John 15:26). The Holy Spirit in us will give us opportunities to share our faith with others so they too will know the good news of Jesus. He will give us strength to stand up for Jesus, sometimes in the midst of hostility.

Showing us the truth

'But when he, the Spirit of truth, comes, he will guide you into all truth. He will not speak on his own; he will speak only what he hears, and he will tell you what is yet to come' (John 16:13). The Holy Spirit will help us to understand more about Jesus, as well as guiding us to know what is right and what is wrong.

Helping us in our weakness and also helping us to pray
'In the same way, the Spirit helps us in our weakness. We do not know what we ought to pray for, but the Spirit himself intercedes for us with groans that words cannot express. And he who searches our hearts knows the mind of the Spirit, because the Spirit intercedes for the saints in accordance with God's will' (Romans 8:26–7). As Christians we don't always know what to pray or even how to pray in certain circumstances. It's at times like this that the Holy Spirit 'intercedes' for us.

Guiding us
'Paul and his companions travelled throughout the region of Phrygia and Galatia, having been kept by the Holy Spirit from preaching the word in the province of Asia' (Acts 16:6). The Holy Spirit will help guide us. We don't really know why in this situation the Holy Spirit told Paul and his colleagues that they shouldn't go into Asia at that particular time. Maybe it was too dangerous. Perhaps something dreadful might have happened. We don't know. But the Holy Spirit guided them, through a word, a prophecy or maybe just a bad gut feeling. That same Holy Spirit wants to help and guide us through our Christian lives.

Convicting us of sin
When he comes, he will convict the world of guilt in regard to sin and righteousness and judgment: in regard to sin, because men do not believe in me; in regard to righteousness, because I am going to the Father, where you can see me no longer; and in regard to judgment, because the prince of this world now stands condemned.
(John 16:8–11)

The Holy Spirit will convict us of our sin and urge us to repent. In short, the Holy Spirit will make us feel bad when we've been bad.

Controversy

There is some controversy about the Holy Spirit, so instead of explaining what different Christian denominations and groups believe, it makes much more sense to see what the Bible actually says.

First, Jesus himself said that the only way to become a Christian is through the Holy Spirit: 'Jesus answered, "I tell you the truth, no one can enter the kingdom of God unless he is born of water and the Spirit" ' (John 3:5). This is Jesus, the Son of God, making it crystal clear that every Christian has received the Holy Spirit. The Apostle Paul, writing some years later to Christians in Rome, reiterates the point in his typically blunt way: 'You, however, are controlled not by the sinful nature but by the Spirit, if the Spirit of God lives in you. And if anyone does not have the Spirit of Christ, he does not belong to Christ' (Romans 8:9). Whether you feel it or not, if you really love Jesus and are a Christian then the Holy Spirit is living in you.

Second, the Holy Spirit is a seal. Not the sort you might see at the zoo catching fish and showing off by balancing a beach ball on the end of its nose, but a guarantee of our place in God's kingdom. A little like a deposit or down-payment you might make to purchase a holiday or a piece of furniture, for example. The New Testament explains it like this: 'And you also were included in Christ when you heard the word of truth, the gospel of your salvation. Having believed, you were marked in him with a seal, the promised Holy Spirit, who is a deposit guaranteeing our inheritance until the redemption of those who are God's possession – to the praise of his glory' (Ephesians 1:13–14). The presence of the Holy Spirit in our lives demonstrates that our faith is very real and proves that we now belong to God

– we are his children, because of what Jesus achieved when he died on the cross.

Third, there's a command running throughout the entire Bible, from the Old Testament right through to the New Testament, that commands us to keep being filled with the Holy Spirit. There's a short list at the end of the chapter for you to look at. To my mind that makes it pretty obvious that it's possible to receive the Holy Spirit, which of course every Christian does when they become a Christian, but also to receive more of the Spirit as well. We all need to keep on being filled with the Holy Spirit because, let's face it, we all leak. We need to be topped up from time to time, and sometimes we might even need to be completely drenched with the Holy Spirit.

Receiving the Holy Spirit

I became a Christian through becoming a member of the Boys' Brigade. I loved playing in the band and taking part in the camping and the expeditions, and could even put up with having to go to church, as there were some nice girls there who I really fancied. I have to admit that the Sunday meetings were a bit of a snore, to put it mildly, and I know if I'd believed in him at all, I would have felt sorry for God having to be there. But that's the downside of omnipresence, I guess. Things did change for me, though, when we went away on a week's camp in glorious sunny Devon.

The leaders spoke about Jesus as if he really had existed, and then told me that God loved me. I decided that if it was true then I most definitely wanted it, and when I got home after our wonderful week under canvas I asked God to come in and change my life. I was now a Christian. Although it was never really explained to me, I believe I was filled with the Holy Spirit at this moment in my Christian life, but it wasn't until some years later that I was really drenched with the power of God.

When it finally happened, I tried to explain my Holy Spirit experience to my elderly Methodist minister. I was surprised, to say the least, by his reaction. He was keen to tell me that this sort of thing didn't happen any more and that it was only for establishing the early Church. That confused me because I knew something wonderful had happened to me, so I went back to the Bible to see what it had to say.

The Bible doesn't say anywhere that the Holy Spirit was just for the very first Christians, and I figured that if the apostles (who, bear in mind, had actually spent three years of their lives with Jesus) needed the Holy Spirit, then I most certainly did too. For some people this experience is very dramatic – some even fall over when the Holy Spirit fills them to overflowing. Others might shake or roar with laughter! For me it happened in my bedroom and it was a very gentle experience. I started to cry and felt very peaceful. I knew something very real had happened and I was never going to be the same again.

The Holy Spirit is for you

Don't miss out on this essential part of being a Christian. It's available for you. Jesus explained: 'How much more will your Father in heaven give the Holy Spirit to those who ask him!' (Luke 11:13). If you honestly feel you've missed out on this step then let me suggest that you get someone to pray with you. Choose someone you trust, who is the same sex as you, and someone who is a more experienced Christian. Then simply ask, believe and receive.

Before we finish this important chapter, just in case you're still wondering, let me tell you what became of the wonder car – the 'amazing' three-wheeled Revette. Well, after the disastrous demonstration, the company swiftly moved to a new factory in Texas where the police began to take an interest in their strange activities. Eventually the officers managed to look around the factory. All they found inside was a pile of rubbish, bits from an old Datsun, a Volkswagen and an old lawnmower. The whole episode was an elaborate moneymaking scam.

Delving deeper

What does the Holy Spirit do in us?
1 John 16:7
2 John 16:9–11
3 John 16:13
4 John 16:14
5 Acts 1:8
6 Romans 8:9
7 Romans 8:16
8 Romans 8:26

What did the Holy Spirit do in the Old Testament?
1 Exodus 31:3
2 Judges 6:34
3 Judges 11:29
4 1 Samuel 10:10
5 1 Samuel 16:13
6 Ezekiel 2:2

Is the Holy Spirit a one-off experience?
1 Joel 2:28–9
2 John 1:33
3 Acts 1:5
4 Ephesians 5:18

How do you receive the Holy Spirit?
1 Luke 3:21–2
2 John 7:37–9
3 Acts 2:4
4 Acts 10:42–6
5 Acts 19:5–6

Memory verse

Jesus answered, 'I tell you the truth, no one can enter the kingdom of God unless he is born of water and the Spirit.'
(John 3:5)

7

Gifts and Fruit
of the Holy Spirit

The Holy Spirit does not obliterate a man's personality; he lifts it to its highest use.

Oswald Chambers

Ephesus was in Turkey and it was Paul's home for just over two years. One day he bumped into some Christians there and had the opportunity to pray for them to receive the Holy Spirit's power. Here's the story of that powerful moment in Paul's own words:

While Apollos was at Corinth, Paul took the road through the interior and arrived at Ephesus. There he found some disciples and asked them, 'Did you receive the Holy Spirit when you believed?'

They answered, 'No, we have not even heard that there is a Holy Spirit.'

So Paul asked, 'Then what baptism did you receive?'

'John's baptism,' they replied.

Paul said, 'John's baptism was a baptism of repentance.

He told the people to believe in the one coming after him, that is, in Jesus.' On hearing this, they were baptised into the name of the Lord Jesus. When Paul placed his hands on them, the Holy Spirit came on them, and they spoke in tongues and prophesied. There were about twelve men in all.

(Acts 19:1–7)

It's clear from this account that these twelve men were believers of sorts. They'd repented of their sins but hadn't yet come to the point of understanding and acting on what Jesus had accomplished when he died and rose again. They also still lacked the power of the Holy Spirit in their lives, so they were struggling. They were incomplete Christians, but they were desperate for more. As Paul prayed for them, they were instantly filled with the Holy Spirit and spoke in different languages and started prophesying. They were now proper Christians.

Gifts

The gifts in the story, speaking in tongues and prophecy, are just two of the many different gifts of the Holy Spirit mentioned in the New Testament. Some of the gifts might be considered more practical, normal and, dare I suggest, mundane, such as teaching or administration, while others are miraculous demonstrations, such as healing and miracles. Whatever the gift or gifts, Paul is clear that they are all good: 'Now to each one the manifestation of the Spirit is given for the common good' (1 Corinthians 12:7). He continues: 'All these are the work of one and the same Spirit, and he gives them to each one, just as he determines' (1 Corinthians 12:11).

They're not to give us special powers so we become spiritual supermen and superwomen. The gifts were given to Christians for the building of the Church, until Jesus comes back again. We read that, when the Holy Spirit came with great force and power at Pentecost, 'you will receive power when the Holy Spirit comes on you; and you will be my witnesses in Jerusalem, and in all Judea and Samaria, and to the ends of the earth' (Acts 1:8). The Holy Spirit came to empower and equip the early Church to take the glorious message of Jesus to their friends and neighbours in the villages and towns around them and to the ends of the earth.

The New Testament lists many gifts, which apart from tongues and interpretation were also seen in the Old Testament from time to time. The main gifts are included in two main passages. It's very interesting that each list is different. No one gift is mentioned on every list and no list has the identical set of gifts. I get the impression that it's almost as if Paul was giving examples as they came to his mind, as opposed to sitting down with pen and paper – or rather, I should say, quill and papyrus – and drawing up an exhaustive list of very specific gifts:

> To one there is given through the Spirit the message of wisdom, to another the message of knowledge by means of the same Spirit, to another faith by the same Spirit, to another gifts of healing by that one Spirit, to another miraculous powers, to another prophecy, to another distinguishing between spirits, to another speaking in different kinds of tongues, and to still another the inter-pretation of tongues. All these are the work of one and the same Spirit, and he gives them to each one, just as he determines.
>
> (1 Corinthians 12:8–11)

The gifts of the Holy Spirit are also listed in this second passage:

> We have different gifts, according to the grace given us. If a man's gift is prophesying, let him use it in proportion to his faith. If it is serving, let him serve; if it is teaching, let him teach; if it is encouraging, let him encourage; if it is

contributing to the needs of others, let him give generously; if it is leadership, let him govern diligently; if it is showing mercy, let him do it cheerfully.

(Romans 12:6–8)

As well as these amazing gifts, there are others listed in other parts of the New Testament. Have a look at these other gifts:

And in the church God has appointed first of all apostles, second prophets, third teachers, then workers of miracles, also those having gifts of healing, those able to help others, those with gifts of administration, and those speaking in different kinds of tongues.

(1 Corinthians 12:28)

There is certainly a degree of overlap between the lists, and indeed Peter's list contains only two gifts which by their very nature seem to encapsulate all the others: 'Each one should use whatever gift he has received to serve others, faithfully administering God's grace in its various forms' (1 Peter 4:10).

Below I've listed the gifts taken from the passages I've mentioned, though I have to admit that throughout the ages Christians have not exactly agreed on how many there are, so please don't treat this list of gifts as exhaustive:

1 Being an apostle – 1 Corinthians 12:28
2 Prophecy – 1 Corinthians 12:28; 1 Corinthians 12:11; Romans 12:6
3 Teaching – 1 Corinthians 12:28; Romans 12:7
4 Miracles – 1 Corinthians 12:28; 1 Corinthians 12:10
5 Healing – 1 Corinthians 12:28; 1 Corinthians 12:9
6 Helping others – 1 Corinthians 12:28
7 Administration – 1 Corinthians 12:28
8 Tongues – 1 Corinthians 12:28; 1 Corinthians 12:10
9 Word of wisdom – 1 Corinthians 12:8

10 Word of knowledge – 1 Corinthians 12:8
11 Faith – 1 Corinthians 12:9
12 Discerning of spirits – 1 Corinthians 12:10
13 Interpreting tongues – 1 Corinthians 12:10
14 Serving – Romans 12:7
15 Encouragement – Romans 12:8
16 Contributing to the needs of others – Romans 12:8
17 Leadership – Romans 12:8
18 Showing mercy – Romans 12:8

That's quite a list, so let me attempt to explain what some of these gifts mean. I won't define all of them as I'm sure many of them, like encouragement, administration and leadership, are pretty obvious anyway. The ones I'm going to unpack could fall into three sub-categories: gifts of knowledge, gifts of power and gifts of communication.

Gifts of knowledge

You get to know someone by spending time with them. I still know some of my old mates from when I was just four years old and in short trousers at infant school. Some thirty years on, I guess there's not much we don't know about each other. In the same way, as we grow in our faith we'll get to know God better, and also we'll learn to hear what he's saying to us. He wants to talk to us so we can get to know him better, but also through the power of the Holy Spirit he wants us to impact the world, so he's given us some very special gifts.

Word of knowledge

This gift has nothing to do with natural knowledge but is supernatural knowledge, revealed by the Holy Spirit, that the recipient would have no way of knowing. There's a great example of this in John's Gospel – John 4:1–29, to be precise. Jesus is having a chat with a woman he's never met before and he uses a number of words of knowledge that enable him to have an amazing conversation with her. To say that she was surprised at his insight and knowledge of her and the sorry state of her life would be a massive understatement: 'Come, see a man who told me everything I ever did. Could this be the Christ?' She was totally gob-smacked!

Word of wisdom

This is a God-given insight into situations. Often a word of wisdom will give divine wisdom and advice after a word of knowledge has brought a problem or difficulty into the light. We frequently need wisdom to know what to do with the knowledge that the Holy Spirit has given us.

Discerning of spirits

This is the ability to recognise spiritual forces at work, sometimes good, sometimes bad. This is a great gift to use during counselling and will help you pray more effectively.

Gifts of power

The power to do miracles comes from the Holy Spirit. Nothing is impossible to God, and often he will intervene in astonishing ways. These gifts work together to glorify Jesus.

Healing

Dramatic demonstrations of healing make up a staggering 90 per cent of the recorded ministry of Jesus on earth. He told his disciples to heal the sick, and after Pentecost we read that they healed people, cast out demons and even raised the dead. We have the same God now, and I know, because I've seen it with my own eyes, that he can heal people today.

Miracles

Miracles are defined as 'marvellous events due to some supposed supernatural agency'. As we've seen from the above, healings would certainly be considered miracles, as would other powerful events that meet a real human need and ultimately bring glory to Jesus. Miracles from the ministry of Jesus that come to mind would include the occasions when he demonstrated power over things, like when he fed the five thousand with the contents of a small boy's lunchbox or when he walked on water. Casting out evil spirits would be another example, as would raising people from the dead, of which there are three accounts in the New Testament.

Faith
Our entire walk with God is based upon faith. A Christian will thank God whether they feel like it or not. Faith is powerful and will give us hope to believe for the impossible. This 'gift of faith' is, I believe, a very special sort of faith for very specific seemingly impossible situations. Jesus demonstrated this sort of faith when he prayed for his close friend, Lazarus, who had been dead for three days. As Jesus exercised his faith there was no doubt in his mind that God was about to do the totally and utterly impossible.

Gifts of communication
God's word is powerful, there's no doubt about that. The Holy Spirit gives supernatural gifts to us to speak the word of God into situations today.

Tongues
Tongues have been described as a 'heart language'. It's the ability to praise God in an unknown language that is spoken to God in prayer or praise. The language might be a human language or an angelic language. Often, 'tongues' are used in worship when you run out of English words to tell God just how flipping fantastic he is. Other times, tongues are used in prayer for situations when you just don't know how to pray. The gift is demonstrated very dramatically in Acts 2:1–13, so maybe take another look at that passage.

Interpreting tongues

I won't insult your intelligence by saying too much about this gift. It's the translation of what is being said when someone speaks in tongues, so that everyone can fully understand. Paul explained that when tongues are used publicly there should be an interpretation, so people know what is going on (1 Corinthians 14:13).

Prophecy

Paul urged us to seek out the gift of prophecy: 'Therefore, my brothers, be eager to prophesy, and do not forbid speaking in tongues' (1 Corinthians 14:39). Prophecy isn't always predicting the future and certainly isn't a private gift that you would use in your bedroom. It's a gift that tells others what God has said, and it's important that other Christians should always weigh up and check what has been prophesied.

As we're all different, God gives us different gifts, though no one gift is more important than another. Paul was straight down the line on that point: 'If the whole body were an eye, where would the sense of hearing be? If the whole body were an ear, where would the sense of smell be? But in fact God has arranged the parts in the body, every one of them, just as he wanted them to be' (1 Corinthians 12:17–18). It's up to you what you do with the gift or gifts that God has given you.

I do believe God gives us gifts not so much for our own sake but for the sake of others. I guess we're like an apple tree that produces fruit, not so we can eat the beautiful juicy apples ourselves but so others can enjoy the results. Your gifts are given so you can bless and encourage others by ministering to them. If you have the gift of teaching, for example, you have it so other Christians will be taught. If you have the gift of hospitality, it is because others will really appreciate the love and the kindness they receive from you. If even one gifted person fails to function and use their gifts properly, then I believe we all miss out.

Fruit

On the subject of apples, as well as talking about receiving gifts the Bible talks about fruit as well. The gifts are a demonstration of the power of God in a person; the fruit is the power of God shown through the life of a person. Back to the imagery of the orchard: a healthy apple tree bears nice juicy apples – good fruit. It's the same with us. The more we are filled with the Holy Spirit, the more we're like Jesus, and this is bound to affect those around who don't yet know Jesus for themselves.

The fruits of being filled with the Holy Spirit are explained in the Bible like this: 'love, joy, peace, patience, kindness, goodness, faithfulness, gentleness and self-control. Against such things there is no law. Those who belong to Christ Jesus have crucified the sinful nature with its passions and desires' (Galatians 5:22–4). Allow me to list these nine fruits as I did earlier with the gifts. The fruit is essential, and these characteristics should shine through every true Christian:

Love
I love my wife and my children. But I also love football and curry. Clearly the latter examples are a different sort of love. The New Testament word used here in this passage for 'love' is *agape*, and it describes God's love for us and the love that God looks for from us. Whatever a person might do to us, we must never seek revenge and we should want nothing more than good for them. It's loving the neighbour who parks in your parking space, or allows their dog to leave a smelly deposit outside your front gate. *Agape* love is a very powerful form of love that involves the will as much as the emotions, the mind as well as the heart.

Joy
Christians should be the most joyful people on earth, yet so often are depicted as old miseries with long faces, square haircuts and black suits, preaching doom and gloom to anyone

unfortunate enough to get in their way. The Christian life should be one of joy. Yes, it's hard sometimes, but Jesus came to give us life. If that's not something to be joyful about, then I don't know what is. Joy is multiplied when it is shared, so go and share some joy.

Peace

It was Billy Graham who said: 'Peace is not arbitrary. It must be based upon definite facts. God has all the facts on his side; the world does not. Therefore God, and not the world, can give peace.' Peace comes from God, and it's not just living cushy lives without hassle and conflict. True peace is the ability to cope with the hard times in life, with the help of the Holy Spirit.

Patience

There's a French proverb that says, 'Patience is bitter, but its fruit is sweet.' My wife will laugh out loud when she reads that I'm writing about patience, as she's convinced I'm the world's most impatient person, particularly when I get behind the wheel of my car. I was really in her bad books recently when our three-year-old daughter shouted, 'Come on, Grandad!' to the elderly driver in front of us who was holding up a great long queue of traffic. My wife figured that Emmie had heard me say that once or twice before and had picked it up herself. Of course, as per usual, she was right. The word 'patience' used in this passage refers to patience with people. Think of the patience God has had with us and make every effort to reproduce this patience with others.

Kindness

A Christian was driving on a lonely country lane one summer day. He saw a car with a flat tyre pulled over on the side of the road. A woman was standing next to the car and looking down in utter dismay at the puncture. The man decided to pull over and show some real Christian kindness. He took off his jacket, rolled up his sleeves and soon grew hot and sweaty and dirty in the sun as he changed the punctured tyre. The woman was watching him, and when he was finished she said, 'Be sure and let the jack down easily now, because my husband is sleeping in the back seat of the car.'

We should show acts of kindness to others whether they deserve it or not. Kindness is an effort, but it's worth it, and generosity and going out of our way for others will have a huge impact.

Goodness

Goodness is love in action. Once again, it's a whole lifestyle mentality. We don't just do good on Sundays or to impress our Christian friends. That is hypocrisy. We shouldn't just wait for extraordinary circumstances to show goodness, we should show goodness to those around us in the ordinary, everyday situation. I love the advice of the preacher Charles Spurgeon: 'Do all the good you can, to all the people you can, in all the ways you can, as often as ever you can, as long as you can.' Do you get the message?

Faithfulness

Faithfulness in lots of little things is a big thing. Faithfulness comes from the word 'faith', and so faithfulness is dependent on faith, and vice versa. I faithfully trust the chef at my local Indian restaurant that my Chicken Dhansak isn't laced with poison. I faithfully accept that the pilot on the aeroplane I'm flying on is fully trained and qualified. We all rely on faithfulness all the time. In people, faithfulness is a great trait. It's a wonderful thing to be able to rely on a person knowing that they won't ever let you down, and that is how Paul is saying we should be.

Gentleness

I'm told by the experts that the Greek word *proates* for 'gentleness' is one of the hardest words to translate. In the New

Testament it has three main meanings: being submissive to the will of God, being teachable, but mostly, being considerate. Many would think gentleness was a trait of being very weak, soft and spineless. But that's not the case. Gentleness includes such great qualities as having strength and being in control, being calm and peaceful when those around you aren't quite so cool and collected.

Self-control

In Scotland many years ago, during the early days of aviation, a stunt pilot was selling rides in his single-engine aeroplane. One day he got into an argument with an old farmer who insisted upon taking his wife along on a trip – at no extra charge. 'Look,' said the pilot finally, 'I'll take you both up for the price of one if you promise not to utter a sound throughout the entire trip. If you make a single sound, the price is doubled.'

They shook hands, the deal was made and they all clambered aboard. The pilot then proceeded to put the aircraft through manoeuvres designed to make the bravest man a gibbering wreck. But, would you believe it, not a sound came from the back where his two passengers sat. Exhausted, he finally set the plane down. As the farmer climbed out, the pilot said, 'I made moves up there that frightened even me, and yet you never said a word. You're a fearless man.'

'I thank ye,' replied the Scotsman. 'But I must admit that there was one time when ye almost had me.'

'And when was that?' asked the pilot.

The farmer replied, 'That was about the time my wife fell out!'

Self-control is concerned with many different areas of our lives, and Paul was describing in his letter to the Galatians (from where the above list is taken) how to be really free. Maybe there are things in your life that need addressing where you need more self-control. It could be dealing with anger, wrong reactions to pressure, overeating or drinking too much, obsessive dieting, watching the wrong things on television. The list could go on and on. I'm not talking about heavy legalism here that makes us feel bad and ties us up, I'm talking about walking in the wonderful freedom of Jesus.

We can try our best to demonstrate these qualities without God's help, but these good intentions will soon wear off. There's nothing we can really do to make them happen ourselves. These fruits are the spontaneous outworking of being filled with the Holy Spirit.

God really does want to fill us all with his Holy Spirit to overflowing, so we can make a significant difference in this world. If that's what you want and it's still not happened, then simply ask God to do it. If you find that hard or want to know more, then ask another Christian to pray for you. Ask someone you know and trust and who knows Jesus better than you do. Receive it in faith and God will do the rest.

Delving deeper

What is the greatest gift?
1 1 Corinthians 13:13

What does the Bible say about the gift of tongues?
1 Acts 2:4
2 Acts 2:11
3 1 Corinthians 14:2
4 1 Corinthians 14:4–5
5 1 Corinthians 14:13–19

How can we grow more fruitful?

1 John 15:4
2 Galatians 5:16
3 Galatians 5:25
4 Colossians 3:2
5 Colossians 3:5–25

Memory verses

Each one should use whatever gift he has received to serve others, faithfully administering God's grace in its various forms. If anyone speaks, he should do it as one speaking the very words of God. If anyone serves, he should do it with the strength God provides, so that in all things God may be praised through Jesus Christ. To him be the glory and the power for ever and ever. Amen.

(1 Peter 4:10–11)

8

Baptism

Baptism seemed such an integral part of New Testament Christianity and I couldn't imagine a droplet of water dribbled on my head when I was a baby could be a proper substitute for that adult symbol of submission and obedience.

Cliff Richard

There is a difference of opinion among evangelical Christians regarding the subject of baptism, but I personally believe baptism is very important. It is certainly not just for those who attend 'Baptist' churches. Baptism was something that Jesus spoke about and indeed commanded the Church to perform as part and parcel of being a true follower of his.

Back to basics

There are two main reasons why Christians should get baptised, or start seriously thinking about it. First, it's because it is something that Jesus did:

> Then Jesus came from Galilee to the Jordan to be baptised by John. But John tried to deter him, saying, 'I need to be

baptised by you, and do you come to me?'

Jesus replied, 'Let it be so now; it is proper for us to do this to fulfil all righteousness.' Then John consented.

As soon as Jesus was baptised, he went up out of the water. At that moment heaven was opened, and he saw the Spirit of God descending like a dove and lighting on him. And a voice from heaven said, 'This is my Son, whom I love; with him I am well pleased.'

(Matthew 3:13–17)

Now, of course, Jesus didn't need to be baptised – after all, he had never committed any sin. He felt he had to do it because in being baptised he was advancing God's work on earth. He was also commending the work that John was doing, as well as identifying with those who desperately needed forgiveness for their sins.

Second, Jesus commanded that all believers be baptised:

Then the eleven disciples went to Galilee, to the mountain where Jesus had told them to go. When they saw him, they worshipped him; but some doubted. Then Jesus came to them and said, 'All authority in heaven and on earth has been given to me. Therefore go and make disciples of all nations, baptising them in the name of the Father and of the Son and of the Holy Spirit, and teaching them to obey everything I have commanded you. And surely I am with you always, to the very end of the age.'

(Matthew 28:16–20)

Bear in mind that these were Jesus' last words, and I would imagine he had chosen his last instructions to his best friends carefully. Look at his four commands again:

1 The disciples were under his authority.

2 They were to make more disciples.
3 They had to baptise and train these new converts to follow him.
4 He would be with them for ever.

It was through these commands that the early Church really began to flourish.

How and why

In the New Testament, baptism was carried out in just one way, by immersion. The person being baptised would be put completely underwater and then (obviously) brought back up again. The Greek word *baptizein* means 'to plunge, dip, immerse' something in water. To me, that seems to suggest more than a sprinkling of water over a person's head.

The Gospel of Mark describes multitudes going to John to be baptised in the River Jordan: 'The whole Judean countryside and all the people of Jerusalem went out to him. Confessing their sins, they were baptised by him in the Jordan River' (Mark 1:5). Later on, the author describes Jesus' own baptism, once again in the very same river. We've already looked at that passage, but refresh yourself again by examining another account of that very special day:

> At that time Jesus came from Nazareth in Galilee and was baptised by John in the Jordan. As Jesus was coming up out of the water, he saw heaven being torn open and the Spirit descending on him like a dove. And a voice came from heaven: 'You are my Son, whom I love; with you I am well pleased.'
>
> (Mark 1:9–11)

The suggestion that Jesus came out of the water strongly suggests that he was immersed, as a sprinkling could have easily been done on the riverbank without Jesus even getting his sandals wet.

Who should be baptised?

The New Testament is very clear about this. Baptism is only for those who have turned from their sins and put Jesus in charge of their lives. Jesus spoke about it and the early Church were keen practitioners. Here are a few more examples from the book of Acts:

> But when they believed Philip as he preached the good news of the kingdom of God and the name of Jesus Christ, they were baptised, both men and women.
>
> (Acts 8:12)

> One of those listening was a woman named Lydia, a dealer in purple cloth from the city of Thyatira, who was a worshipper of God. The Lord opened her heart to respond to Paul's message. When she and the members of her household were baptised, she invited us to her home.
>
> (Acts 16:14–15)

> They replied, 'Believe in the Lord Jesus, and you will be saved – you and your household.' Then they spoke the word of the Lord to him and to all the others in his house. At that hour of the night the jailer took them and washed their wounds; then immediately he and all his family were baptised. The jailer brought them into his house and set a meal before them; he was filled with joy because he had come to believe in God – he and his whole family.
>
> (Acts 16:31–4)

Those are just three examples – there are many others. In the New Testament, baptism was a sign of being cleansed from wrong-doing and starting an exciting new life with Jesus. That's why some Christians aren't so keen when it comes to infant baptism. The subject of the baptism of babies isn't mentioned anywhere in the Bible, though certain denominations would see the sprinkling of water over the head of babies as symbolic of the sprinkled blood of Jesus when he died on the cross. I agree it's a wonderful thing to dedicate these little ones to God and to celebrate their arrival into the world with a church service for the family, followed by a mushroom vol-au-vent and a small glass of sherry, but I believe Jesus was talking about a different sort of baptism.

Significance of baptism

There's a lot of important symbolism involved in baptism. The Apostle Paul told the Christians in Rome:

> What shall we say, then? Shall we go on sinning, so that grace may increase? By no means! We died to sin; how can we live in it any longer? Or don't you know that all of us who were baptised into Christ Jesus were baptised into his death? We were therefore buried with him through baptism into death in order that, just as Christ was raised from the dead through the glory of the Father, we too may live a new life.
>
> (Romans 6:1–4)

When Jesus died on the cross, he didn't just die to set us free from our sins. He also died in our place, for all the things we do, say and think that are wrong. He became our representative. Paul was saying that when we get baptised it's like a symbol of Jesus' own death and resurrection.

On another occasion, while under house arrest in Rome, Paul wrote similar words to the Christians in Colosse: 'having been buried with him in baptism and raised with him through your faith in the power of God, who raised him from the dead' (Colossians 2:12). In Paul's day, immersion was the only form of baptism practised. The new Christians were 'buried' when they went under the water. It symbolised the death, and indeed burial, of their old lives, and when they came out of the water it symbolised a resurrection into a new and exciting life with Jesus. Once again, a mere sprinkling would destroy this vivid imagery.

I've mentioned already that Jesus commanded baptism, as did the apostles: 'Peter replied, "Repent and be baptised, every one of you, in the name of Jesus Christ for the forgiveness of your sins. And you will receive the gift of the Holy Spirit" ' (Acts 2:38). It is clearly important, but I don't believe essential, for becoming a Christian. In other words, you can be a true follower of Jesus without being baptised.

Jesus' statement to a dying thief who was crucified alongside him backs this up: 'Jesus answered him, "I tell you the truth, today you will be with me in paradise" ' (Luke 23:43). The thief had asked for forgiveness and became a Christian that day, though obviously didn't have the opportunity to be baptised. So clearly baptism isn't absolutely essential, but if we're to be obedient to Jesus then it is important.

At the end of the day, baptism is an outward sign of an inner commitment to follow Jesus. It's a very public sign that you are finishing with your old life and entering into a new life with Jesus at the very centre. Don't miss out on it.

Delving deeper

What does baptism signify?
1 Acts 22:16
2 Romans 6:1–4
3 Romans 6:4–5
4 1 Corinthians 12:13
5 Galatians 3:27

When should a new Christian be baptised?

1 Matthew 3:6
2 Acts 2:41
3 Acts 16:33

Is it really necessary to be baptised?

1 Matthew 28:19
2 Acts 2:38
3 Acts 10:48

Memory verses

Or don't you know that all of us who were baptised into Christ Jesus were baptised into his death? We were therefore buried with him through baptism into death in order that, just as Christ was raised from the dead through the glory of the Father, we too may live a new life.

(Romans 6:3–4)

9

Church

The Christian church is a society of sinners. It is the only society in the world in which membership is based upon the single qualification that the candidate shall be unworthy of membership.

Charles Clayton Morrison

A couple woke up one Sunday morning and the wife got dressed for church. It was just about time for the service when she noticed her husband hadn't even got out of bed. Rather puzzled, she asked, 'Why aren't you getting ready for church?'

He said, 'Because I don't want to go.'

She thought he might be ill or something, so she asked, 'Why not?'

He said, 'Well, there's three reasons really. First, everyone is so unfriendly. Second, no one likes me. And third, I just don't want to go.'

The wife replied, 'Well, darling, I have three reasons why you should go. First, most of the people are friendly. Second, there are one or two people who like you. And third, you're the vicar! So get dressed!'

I guess if I'd been given £1 every time I've been asked the

question, 'Do I have to go to church to be a Christian?' I'd be basking on a beach in the Bahamas right now, instead of sitting here typing in overcast, drizzly Littlehampton. The answer to the $64,000 question is quite simply 'no'. You don't have to go to church to be a Christian. And for that matter, as I said before, going to church doesn't make you a Christian any more than going to McDonald's makes you a hamburger. So it's not an automatic thing, but having said that, going to a church is a very important part of your Christian growth. In actual fact, you don't *go to* church, you *become part of* a church – and that's quite an important difference.

When I was small I used to play football in our garden by myself, kicking the ball against the side of our house and passing it back – it kept me occupied for hours on end. But the best way to play football was on a Saturday afternoon with the rest of the team. Once you've become a Christian, you become part of the church team, and also part of a new family of around 1.5 billion men, women and children across the world. It's good to spend time with your new family – though obviously not all at the same time.

The author C.S. Lewis quickly realised he'd find it hard to live the Christian faith without others. This is what he observed:

> When I first became a Christian, about fourteen years ago, I thought that I could do it on my own, by retiring to my rooms and reading theology, and I wouldn't go to the churches and gospel halls. I disliked very much their hymns, which I considered to be fifth-rate poems set to sixth-rate music. But as I went on I saw the great merit of it. I came up against different people of quite different outlooks and different education, and then gradually my conceit just began peeling off. I realised that the hymns (which were just sixth-rate music) were, nevertheless, being sung with devotion and benefit by an old saint in elastic-sided boots

in the opposite pew, and then you realise that you aren't fit to clean those boots.

I want to be honest with you and admit that some church meetings are really boring, and won't help you much at all. Unfortunately, some are little more than hymn-singing clubs. At one particularly dull church one morning, one seven-year-old boy suddenly asked his Sunday School teacher, 'When can we go home? This is so boring!'

Immediately the little girl to his left shoved him and snapped at him, 'Shut up. It's supposed to be boring!'

Having said that, loads of churches are brilliant. Find one that's good, with friendly welcoming people who love God, read and study the Bible in a helpful way and are passionate about reaching those who aren't Christians and don't yet know Jesus.

What the Church is really like

Jesus loved the Church so much he gave his life: 'Husbands, love your wives, just as Christ loved the church and gave himself up for her' (Ephesians 5:25). So important is the Church that God has put Jesus in charge of it: 'And God placed all things under his feet and appointed him to be head over everything for the church, which is his body, the fulness of him who fills everything in every way' (Ephesians 1:22–3).

The Bible uses a variety of images to describe what the Church is like. Paul referred to the Church as the bride of Christ as he explained that a relationship between a husband and a wife can be likened to Jesus and the Church:

> After all, no one ever hated his own body, but he feeds and cares for it, just as Christ does the church – for we are members of his body. 'For this reason a man will leave his father and mother and be united to his wife, and the two

will become one flesh.' This is a profound mystery – but I am talking about Christ and the church.

(Ephesians 5:30–2)

One of my favourite images used is that of a family. Paul wrote to one of his closest friends, Timothy, who was a young leader of a church. He was giving practical advice on how he should help people in his church, by treating them as family: 'Do not rebuke an older man harshly, but exhort him as if he were your father. Treat younger men as brothers, older women as mothers, and younger women as sisters, with absolute purity' (1 Timothy 5:1–2). By using that lovely family image, it's crystal clear that when we meet together as church we should invest time, fun and fellowship, and love one another.

The first local church

The first ever church was far from boring. In the New Testament the word 'church' never actually meant an old building with a steeple and pews and a graveyard in the grounds. Indeed, it didn't mean any sort of building, and the actual Greek word for church, *ekklesia*, simply meant 'the called-out ones' or, put another way, 'people of like mind and vision'. The first local church was like this. It numbered over three thousand new Christians who became believers after the Apostle Peter had preached the gospel message in Jerusalem:

They devoted themselves to the apostles' teaching and to the fellowship, to the breaking of bread and to prayer. Everyone was filled with awe, and many wonders and miraculous signs were done by the apostles. All the believers were together and had everything in common. Selling their possessions and goods, they gave to anyone as he had need. Every day they continued to meet together in the temple courts. They broke bread in their homes and ate together with glad and sincere hearts, praising God and enjoying the favour of all the people. And the Lord added to their number daily those who were being saved.

(Acts 2:42–7)

That certainly doesn't sound boring to me.

The new Christians learned together in a wonderful spirit of friendship and camaraderie. They prayed for God to give them strength in their lives and they in turn saw God do some awesome miracles in the process. They shared all they had with each other and with those in their community in real need, and they worshipped God. Finally, and very significantly, they were so happy (v. 46) and their church was so attractive that it drew others. I guess outsiders couldn't help liking what they saw, so they came and experienced it for themselves and met God along the way.

The structure of the early Church

Look around your town and you will see many different churches: Baptist, Church of England, Methodist, Salvation Army, House Church, URC, Evangelical Free Church, Pentecostal, Catholic, Brethren . . . the list goes on and on. Sadly, few seem to have much in common and they often have little to do with each other. This is so different from the New Testament Church which, although spread across many different villages, towns and even countries in the Middle East, was united in its beliefs and the way it lived out those beliefs.

Jesus is the 'head' of the Church. Paul describes the rest of the 'body' as follows:

It was he who gave some to be apostles, some to be prophets, some to be evangelists, and some to be pastors and teachers, to prepare God's people for works of service, so that the body of Christ may be built up until we all reach unity in the faith and in the knowledge of the Son of God and become mature, attaining to the whole measure of the fulness of Christ.

(Ephesians 4:11–13)

You may remember that this very same passage is one that we looked at earlier when we examined the gifts of the Holy Spirit. It's an important list because it's the model of church that Jesus said should operate 'until' (v. 13) we reach unity in the faith. Most of us are familiar with terms like 'vicar', 'minister', 'priest', 'rector' and 'archbishop' although many of them aren't mentioned in the Bible. So let's take a closer look at the list that is mentioned and what the terms mean:

1 *Apostles*: 'apostle' means 'one sent out' as a messenger or missionary. The word soon became an official title for Jesus' twelve disciples after his death and resurrection (Acts 1:25–6 and Ephesians 2:20).
2 *Prophets*: prophets are found throughout the entire Bible. Their important job was to bring God's word to the churches and to train them in the Scriptures. Sometimes they even predicted the future.
3 *Evangelists*: these people have a special gift of preaching the gospel and seeing people become Christians. Philip was an example of an evangelist in the Bible (Acts 8) and Billy Graham is probably the most effective evangelist of the modern age.
4 *Pastors*: the Latin word *pastor* means 'shepherd'. The shepherd of Jesus' day would walk in front of his precious flock, keeping them from harm and danger and looking for the best food and shelter he could find. Jesus is the ultimate 'good shepherd': 'I am the good shepherd. The good shepherd lays down his life for the sheep' (John 10:11).
5 *Teachers*: pretty obvious, really. Surprise, surprise, these were those chosen to teach and instruct others in the ways of

God. We all need help as we grow in Jesus in many different aspects of our faith, and teachers are the men and women to help do the job.

So, to reiterate, that was the model suggested by Jesus, the 'head' of the Church, and his authority was to be exercised by apostles, prophets, evangelists, pastors and teachers. The first three 'ministries', then and now, tended to have more of a travelling role, while pastors and teachers would almost always be linked and based at a local church.

The structure of the Church today

The local church is the church near you where other believers meet to worship God. The leader is likely to be a pastor or teacher, and may be called that or may use the term 'vicar', 'minister' or whatever. Either way, they should be a person who loves God, loves and cares for their flock – which includes, of course, you – and has a deep desire to serve others.

Other churches may have elders instead. They often operate in a team and are responsible for the church and the general direction of church life. It may be their full-time job or not. They often have deacons helping them with the more practical aspects of running the church, with administration, finance, putting chairs out, buildings maintenance, etc. Irrespective of precise or definitive titles, the role of leadership in the church is important and the biblical standards are high:

An elder must be blameless, the husband of but one wife, a man whose children believe and are not open to the charge of being wild and disobedient. Since an overseer is entrusted with God's work, he must be blameless – not overbearing, not quick-tempered, not given to drunkenness, not violent, not pursuing dishonest gain. Rather he must be hospitable, one who loves what is good, who is self-controlled, upright, holy and disciplined. He must hold firmly to the trustworthy message as it has been taught, so that he can encourage others by sound doctrine and refute those who oppose it.

(Titus 1:6–9)

Unless the church you go to is very small, it is unlikely that the main leader will be able to shepherd the whole flock. Not that they wouldn't want to, it's just that they practically wouldn't have the hours in the day, or the days in the week to do the job properly. Many churches put their members into smaller groups that meet midweek to study, learn, pray, eat and drink, care and laugh together. These are called house groups, cells, house fellowships, home groups or whatever, and it is something that the New Testament seemed to do a lot of. The home group is a great place to spend quality time with other believers and ask all the tricky questions you might feel embarrassed to ask during a larger and more formal meeting.

The role of the Church

Worshipping together with other Christians is powerful. It's much more than singing some ancient hymns with an equally antiquated organ – or, indeed, belting out very modern songs to the accompaniment of folk guitars and out-of-rhythm tambourines. Worship is more than just padding the service out or giving people the chance to stand up and stretch their legs and exercise their vocal cords. Paul commended the church in Colosse to 'sing psalms, hymns and spiritual songs with gratitude in your hearts to God' (Colossians 3:16). God loves our worship.

As well as worship, the Church has another vital role to play in caring for Christians and building them up in their faith: 'We proclaim him, admonishing and teaching everyone with all wisdom, so that we may present everyone perfect in Christ' (Colossians 1:28). The word 'perfect' used in this translation means mature. Definitely not perfect. Paul knew that the only way the Church could be really effective was for Christians to grow into wisdom and maturity in their faith. It's not enough just to see people come to a personal faith in Jesus, though of course that is absolutely wonderful. The goal of the Church should be to make these new Christians and every Christian 'mature' in Jesus.

Finally, and equally important, is for every church to have a focus and heart for reaching the lost – those who don't yet know Jesus for themselves: 'Therefore go and make disciples of all nations, baptising them in the name of the Father and of the Son and of the Holy Spirit' (Matthew 28:19). This evangelistic edge should always be coupled with social action as we care for the poor, needy and downtrodden in the name of Jesus. Imagine the impact this will have on our local communities as they see Jesus through our kind words and actions. Jesus' instructions couldn't have been easier to understand: 'But love your enemies, do good to them, and lend to them without expecting to get anything back. Then your reward will be great, and you will be sons of the Most High, because he is kind to the ungrateful and wicked. Be merciful, just as your Father is merciful' (Luke 6:35–6). 'Love' in these verses means action. Worship, looking after each other and practical help coupled with evangelism can have a profound effect on our communities, will raise the profile of Jesus and your church, and will in time see many people turn to him.

Your part in the local church

We've seen that church isn't a building, but people of like mind and vision. The Church is a family and, from the youngest to the oldest, from the most experienced to the newest baby Christian, all have an important role to play in that family.

We've already examined different images used for the Church. The Apostle Paul often used the analogy of the human body to teach how the Church should get on together, in spite and because of our different gifts. Look carefully at his words to the church in Rome:

> For by the grace given me I say to every one of you: Do not think of yourself more highly than you ought, but rather think of yourself with sober judgment, in accordance with the measure of faith God has given you. Just as each of us has one body with many members, and these members do not all have the same function, so in Christ we who are many form one body, and each member belongs to all the others. We have different gifts, according to the grace given us. If a man's gift is prophesying, let him use it in proportion to his faith. If it is serving, let him serve; if it is teaching, let him teach; if it is encouraging, let him encourage; if it is contributing to the needs of others, let him give generously; if it is leadership, let him govern diligently; if it is showing mercy, let him do it cheerfully.
>
> (Romans 12:3–8)

That should be a great manifesto for us all. You might not be a great prophet (yet) but you could serve others by offering really practical, down-to-earth help. A lift to church, for example, gardening for an elderly neighbour, shopping for a housebound friend, some painting and decorating for someone who desperately needs it. Whatever you do, let it be the best you can possibly do. General William Booth, founder of the Salvation Army, was asked the secret of his amazing Christian life. Booth answered, 'I told the Lord that he could have all that there is of William Booth.' What a great philosophy on life and service to others.

Commenting on the gift of encouragement – 'if it is encouraging, let him encourage' (v. 8) – William Barclay, the Bible scholar, made this point:

One of the highest of human duties is the duty of encouragement. It is easy to pour cold water on their enthusiasm; it is easy to discourage others. The world is full of discouragers. We have a Christian duty to encourage one another. Many a time a word of praise or thanks or appreciation or cheer has kept a man on his feet.

Encouragement is something we can all do and it can make such a difference. The power of encouragement and motivation is well known in business. Indeed, it's been proven that a motivator will make it to the top before a genius. Many years ago, when Andrew Carnegie hired Charles Schwab to administer his far-flung steel empire, Schwab became the first man in history to earn a million dollars a year while in someone else's employment. Schwab was once asked what equipped him to earn $3,000 a day (a lot of money now, let alone then). Was it his knowledge of steel manufacturing? 'Nonsense,' said Schwab. 'I have lots of men working for me who know more about steel than I do.' Schwab was paid such a huge amount largely because of his ability to inspire other people. 'I consider my ability to arouse enthusiasm among the men the greatest asset I possess,' he said, 'and any person who can do that can go almost anywhere and name almost any price.' Encouragement is powerful, so do it.

Finally, be yourself at church. A little old man was seen every Sunday morning walking to church. He was deaf, so he could not hear a word of the sermon, or the music sung by the choir, or the hymns sung by the congregation. A cynic asked, 'Why do you spend your Sundays in that church when you can't hear a word?' He replied, 'I want my neighbours to know which side I'm on.' Don't be something you're not and don't do or say things to impress others. God wants you to be honest, so be vulnerable to God and those new friends that you trust at church, and enjoy growing in God with your new family.

Delving deeper

What did the early Church do when they met in smaller groups?
1 Acts 2:46
2 Acts 12:12
3 Acts 16:40
4 Romans 16:4–5
5 1 Corinthians 16:19

How did people join the early Church?
1 Acts 2:41
2 Acts 4:32
3 Acts 5:13

See how the early Church grew so fast. Is there anything we can learn from them?
1 Acts 1:15
2 Acts 2:41
3 Acts 3:4
4 Acts 5:14
5 Acts 6:7
6 Acts 12:24

Memory verses

It was he who gave some to be apostles, some to be prophets, some to be evangelists, and some to be pastors and teachers, to prepare God's people for works of service, so that the body of Christ may be built up until we all reach unity in the faith and in the knowledge of the Son of God and become mature, attaining to the whole measure of the fulness of Christ.

(Ephesians 4:11–13)

10

Bible

You Christians have in your keeping a document with enough dynamite in it to blow the whole of civilisation to bits; to turn this world upside down; to bring peace to this war-torn world. But you read it as if it were just good literature, and nothing else.

Mahatma Gandhi

The Bible is astonishing. It has been banned, burned and beloved. It has been read by more people than any other book in the history of the world. It is presented to kings and queens at coronations, to presidents when they are sworn in, and to witnesses in courts of law. It has been attacked more than any other book in history, with generations attempting to discredit it. It has been carried into prison cells and smuggled into countries where it is outlawed by evil dictators, yet I would wager it gathers more dust on more shelves than any other book.

It is certainly a remarkable book. I don't suppose many people walking into a book store while shopping on a Saturday afternoon and asking for the world's best-selling book would expect to be sold the Bible. But it is true. The Bible is the world's number one best-seller, and is quite an amazing book. The Bible (or portions of it) has been published in 1,783 languages and dialects and is currently available in the languages of 97 per cent of the world's people. The United Bible Societies of America and Europe now distribute 500,000,000 Bibles a year.

The book from God

Christians believe that the Bible is very special because it is the word of God. Just three verses into Genesis we see the words 'And God said'. Depending on the translation of the Bible you are using, this phrase or variations on it, like 'thus says the Lord', runs throughout the Old Testament and is used literally hundreds of times. So if you believe that, then the words in the Bible are God's very own words.

Although the book was written by people, these men and women were inspired by God, meaning that ultimately God was the author of the Bible. Obviously they wrote from their own personal, historical and cultural perspectives, but they wrote what God wanted them to write. The Bible says of itself: 'All Scripture is God-breathed and is useful for teaching, rebuking, correcting and training in righteousness' (2 Timothy 3:16).

When you want to get to know someone you spend time with them. If that's not possible – because of geographical difficulties, for example – you might try to write a letter or send an e-mail or talk to them on the telephone. Maybe, for whatever reason, that's not possible either, so perhaps you might try to find out more about them from a book, as you would a celebrity or a famous historical person. God gave us the Bible so we could know more about him and his will for our lives.

Bible facts

The actual word 'Bible' comes from the Greek word *biblia*, meaning 'books'. It is made up of sixty-six books in one, written over a 1,500-year period by over forty authors: fishermen, soldiers, kings, peasants, philosophers and even Daniel, a prime minister. The Bible was written in three languages, Hebrew, Aramaic and Greek, and includes history books, biographies, poems, songs and even a book of love letters. For all its diversity, however, the Bible is a unit. From beginning to end it tells the story of God's plan for friendship with mankind, which people got wrong and Jesus made right.

The Bible is split into two Testaments, the Old and the New, with the word 'Testament' meaning 'covenant' or 'promise'. The Old Testament was written before Jesus came and, put very simply, is about God's dealings with Israel. It was written in Hebrew for the most part, as this was the language of the Jewish people, and was obviously the only Bible that the early Church had during Jesus' day and for some twenty years afterwards. The Old Testament looked forward to Jesus' coming; the New Testament tells of his arrival on earth and of his life and teaching, and includes the writings of his followers.

The Old Testament

The Old Testament was, of course, the Bible that the early Church used. It was written mainly in Palestine, covers some two thousand years and is made up of thirty-nine books – seventeen historical books, five poetic books, and finishing with seventeen prophetic books. The Old Testament is a story of a group of travelling tribesmen who later became the nation of Israel. Famous incidents and characters in the Old Testament that you may already recognise include:

1 The creation of the world
2 Adam and Eve
3 Noah and the flood
4 Abraham
5 Isaac
6 Jacob

7 Joseph
8 Moses
9 Crossing the Red Sea
10 The Ten Commandments
11 Joshua
12 Gideon
13 Samson
14 David and Goliath
15 Two kingdoms – Israel and Judah
16 The Jews' return to Jerusalem

All in all, it's a cracking good read full of murder, mystery, sex and suspense and would make an awesome Hollywood block-buster. Between the end of the Old Testament and the start of the New Testament there is a time-scale of around four hundred years, and by this time the Romans were the great world superpower.

The New Testament

The New Testament contains twenty-seven separate books that were all written in the first century AD, less than seventy years after Jesus' death. They contain the story of his life and the beginnings of the Christian Church from around 4 BC. The New Testament is made up of five historical books: the four Gospels – Matthew, Mark, Luke and John, which tell of the life of Jesus from four different perspectives – and the book of Acts, which tells the exciting story of how the early Church started.

The facts were recorded by eyewitnesses, who gave first-hand accounts of what they had seen and heard: 'That which was from the beginning, which we have heard, which we have seen with our eyes, which we have looked at and our hands have touched – this we proclaim concerning the Word of life' (1 John 1:1).

The New Testament also contains 'epistles'. A friend of mine really did think that the epistles were the wives of the apostles. But they are letters, and of the twenty-one letters in the New Testament, thirteen were written by Paul. The New Testament finishes with a prophetic book called Revelation.

The Apocrypha

You may also have heard of the Apocrypha, so let me explain a little about it. During the period between the completion of the Old Testament and the first writings included in the New Testament (i.e. the period between 450 BC and AD 50), many essays, psalms and historical accounts circulated throughout the synagogues and early churches. These writings were given the name 'Apocrypha' (meaning 'hidden'). Though they are all from the time before the birth of Jesus, they were never included in the Hebrew Bible. However, many Christians found the teachings helpful and in some editions of the Bible they were included among the Old Testament books.

Then Martin Luther, in his Bible translation of 1534, removed the apocryphal books from their usual places in the Old Testament, and instead had them printed at the end of the Old Testament. He stated that they 'are not held equal to the Sacred Scriptures and yet are useful and good for reading'. After that, many Protestant Bibles omitted them completely. However, in 1546 the Roman Catholic Council of Trent specifically listed the apocryphal books approved by the Roman Catholic Church as inspired by God, and they are always included in Roman Catholic Bibles, usually interspersed among the books of the Old Testament.

The Apocrypha generally consists of fourteen booklets, of which 1 and 2 Maccabees and 1 Esdras are the main documents and form the bulk of the apocryphal writings. The first book of Maccabees is a historical account of the struggle of the Maccabee family and their followers for Jewish independence from 167 to 134 BC. Basically, 2 Maccabees covers the same ground but dramatises the accounts and includes moral teaching. Other books are Tobit, Judith, Baruch, Ecclesiasticus, and The Wisdom of Solomon.

Since neither Jesus nor the apostles make any reference to the apocryphal books, most Christians have regarded their authority as secondary to that of the thirty-nine books of the Old Testament and they are not included in most Bibles.

How the Bible came together

The sixty-six books that make up the Bible are known as the 'canon of Scripture'. 'Canon' means 'general law or principle', and the canon books are those that the Church, through much discussion and prayer, accepted as being the inspired word of God.

No one church created the canon, but a number of churches and councils gradually accepted the list of books recognised by Christian believers everywhere as being inspired. It wasn't actually until AD 367 that the church father Athanasius first provided the complete listing of the sixty-six books belonging to the Bible. He noted that these sixty-six books were the only ones universally accepted.

The eminent scholar F. F. Bruce was clearly impressed by the Bible. This is what he observed:

> The Bible, at first sight, appears to be a collection of literature – mainly Jewish. If we enquire into the circumstances under which the various Biblical documents were written, we find that they were written at intervals over a space of nearly 1,600 years. The writers wrote in various lands, from Italy in the west to Mesopotamia and possibly Persia in the east. The writers themselves were a heterogeneous [I had to look this up – it means 'diverse in character'] number of people, not only separated from each other by hundreds of years and hundreds of miles, but

belonging to the most diverse walks of life. In their ranks we have kings, herdsmen, soldiers, legislators, fishermen, statesmen, courtiers, priests and prophets, a tent-making Rabbi and a Gentile physician, not to speak of others of whom we know nothing apart from the writings they have left us. The writings themselves belong to a great variety of literary types. They include history, law (civil, criminal, ethical, ritual, sanitary), allegory, biography, personal correspondence, personal memoirs and diaries.

Bruce continues, 'For all that, the Bible is not simply an anthology; there is a unity which binds the whole together. An anthology is compiled by an anthologist, but no anthologist compiled the Bible.'

These are important words from someone who really knows what he's talking about. It just goes to show how unique the Bible is. Let's take a very brief look at how it was physically written. The Jews preserved the manuscript as no other manuscript had ever been preserved. The original biblical manuscripts would have been written on to papyrus, parchments, vellum (calf skin), stone, clay and wax tablets, using pointed reed pens or chisels. The manuscripts were then copied with meticulous care and accuracy. The Jews had special groups of men whose sole duty was to preserve and reproduce the original manuscripts. They took their job very seriously – even the tiniest and most insignificant error would mean the whole manuscript would be destroyed and they would have to start over again.

The New Testament soon became the most frequently copied and widely circulated book of the ancient world. There are currently 24,633 manuscript copies or portions of the New Testament in existence, compared with just ten and seven copies for Julius Caesar and Plato respectively. You can see what a huge difference that is. Author John Robinson wrote, 'The wealth of manuscripts, and above all the narrow interval and time between the writing and the earliest extant copies, make it by far the best attested text of any ancient writing in the world.'

A book worth dying for

We have the English Bible because of scholars like John Wycliffe and William Tyndale. Tyndale, for example, finally finished translating the Bible into English in July 1525 and throughout his life faced intense opposition for doing so. His life would have made even the most thrilling James Bond movie seem dull, as he faced narrow escapes and numerous action-packed adventures along the way. But on 16th October 1536 he was finally caught and strangled to death. Then, for good measure, his captors burned his body at the stake. His enemies must have thought that was the end of Tyndale and his Bible, but they were so wrong. The product of his labours, the English Bible, is with us today – a book that William Tyndale certainly thought was well worth dying for.

The importance of the Bible

You may agree that all this is very admirable, but why do we need the Bible today? As well as its being a great handbook for life, I think reading and understanding the Bible is important for a number of reasons.

It nourishes

Just as food and drink nourishes our physical bodies, so our spiritual bodies are fed by the words of God we read in the Bible: 'Jesus answered, "It is written: 'Man does not live on bread alone, but on every word that comes from the mouth of God' " ' (Matthew 4:4). If we stopped eating and drinking for a long period of time, it would seriously harm our bodies and eventually end in death. Jesus is urging us not to neglect reading the Bible, for doing so would harm our souls.

It gives instruction

The Bible gives clear instructions for us to live our lives in a way that pleases God. We don't know everything about God, but he has given us enough information through the words of the Bible for us to know his plans for our lives. The Bible has been described as 'God's chart for us to steer by, to keep us from the bottom of the sea, and to show us where the harbour is, and how to reach it without running on rocks'. We often see the slogan 'For best results, follow maker's instructions' on products in the High Street. It's exactly the same with the Bible. Read it and follow its instructions and it will be the best manual for life.

It reveals more of Jesus

The English painter J.M.W. Turner invited Charles Kingsley to his studio to see a picture of a storm at sea. In total admiration, Kingsley exclaimed, 'It's wonderful. It's so realistic. How did you do it?'

The artist replied, 'I went to the coast of Holland and paid a fisherman to take me out to sea in the next storm. Entering his boat as a storm was brewing, I asked him to bind me to the mast. Then he steered his boat into the teeth of the storm. The storm raged with such fury that at times I longed to be in the bottom of the boat where the waves would blow over me. I could not, however. I was bound to the mast. Not only did I see the storm in its raging fury, I felt it. It blew into me, as it were, until I became a part of it. After this terrible ordeal, I returned to my studio and painted the picture.'

In the same way, Jesus came to our earth to experience real life for himself. He got hungry and thirsty, he loved people and he loved to help them. He was killed to take away the sin of the world, so that we could know him. The whole Bible, from cover to cover, is built around this wonderful story and the promise of a hope and a future for those who choose to follow him.

Getting the most out of the Bible

Recently in the hit TV series *The Simpsons*, the father of the dysfunctional cartoon family, Homer Simpson, described the Bible as a 2,000-page sleeping-pill! I guess, if I'm honest, when I first became a Christian I did find reading the Bible a little boring from time to time. In fact, if I'm really honest, sometimes I still find it hard going these days, and I don't think I'm the only one. I also have to admit that understanding the Bible doesn't automatically become a doddle when you become a Christian, so please don't feel abnormal or under pressure if you do find it a little difficult. Join the club.

It might seem a strange thing to say, but when it comes to actually reading the Bible, the beginning might not be the best place to start. The Old Testament tells us how God helped and guided people in the past, while the New Testament tells us of Jesus' birth and beyond. So as you start to follow Jesus, why not get to know him a little more by reading the Gospels: Matthew, Mark, Luke and John, four different authors who tell us the life story of Jesus from their perspectives. Here are some other suggestions that might help:

1 Get a modern translation. There are many different versions of the Bible, and if you get confused by 'thee's' and 'thou's' then I suggest you get your hands on a modern translation of the Bible, something that is easier for you to understand.

2 Get a small pocket-sized version as well if you can afford it. It's great for sticking in your pocket (as the name might suggest) and reading at any time of the day or night when you've got some spare time. I keep a small Bible in my car, and I always try to read it when I'm hanging around while I'm waiting for one of my children, or for my wife to return from one of her shopping expeditions.

3 Read the Bible with an open mind. Try to read and study

fairly and honestly and ask God to speak to you through what you read.

4 Consider using Bible study notes. There are loads available at your local Christian bookshop, with versions suitable for all ages as well as for brand new Christians. I have used notes to study the Bible and have personally found them very useful.

5 Make notes. If you find a verse or story or something that particularly speaks to you, then jot it down in a notebook or even mark it in your Bible. Likewise, if you find something you don't understand, then make a note of it and ask another Christian what it means.

6 Get into a routine. Some habits are good and some are bad – we all know that. Setting regular time aside at a certain time each day to read your Bible is very important and a very good habit. Please don't feel that getting up at 4 a.m. to study the Scriptures is more spiritual than reading your Bible before you go to bed. Be flexible. The important thing is that you do it consistently.

7 Meditate on what you read. I'm not suggesting that we empty our minds, the way many Eastern religions suggest. Meditation is finding a quiet place and chewing over a piece of Scripture and seeing what God says through it.

8 Memorise verses. Learning favourite verses is a very good principle for our Christian lives. As we meditate on God's words, let's believe we become more like God.

Finally, do you know how much time it would take to read from Genesis to Revelation? If you read the Bible at a normal speed (slow enough to be heard and understood) the reading time would be seventy-one hours. If you broke that down into minutes and divided it into 365 days, you could read the entire Bible in a year, cover to cover, in only twelve minutes a day. That's not much time, is it, to spend reading about God? Maybe that's a target you should set for yourself.

Delving deeper

Why was the Bible given to us?
1 John 20:31
2 2 Timothy 3:16
3 1 John 5:13

What did Jesus say about the Scriptures?
1 Matthew 4:4
2 Matthew 5:17–18
3 Luke 24:44
4 John 10:35

Is the Bible the word of God?
1 Hosea 1:1
2 Joel 1:1
3 2 Peter 1:20–1
4 2 Timothy 3:15–17

Why is it important to read the Bible?
1 Psalm 119:11
2 Psalm 119:18
3 Psalm 119:34
4 Psalm 119:103
5 Psalm 119:105

Memory verse

All Scripture is God-breathed and is useful for teaching, rebuking, correcting and training in righteousness.

(2 Timothy 3:16)

11

Prayer

A man without prayer is like a tree without roots.

Pope Pius XII

Once upon a time there was a man who went hunting for bears in Canada. As he trudged through the forest he reached a large and steep hill. He climbed the hill and, just as he was pulling himself up over the last outcrop of rocks, a huge bear met him nose to nose. The bear roared fiercely. The man was so scared that he lost his balance and fell down the hill, with the bear following in hot pursuit not far behind.

On the trip down the hill the man lost his gun. When he finally stopped tumbling, he found that he had a broken leg. Escape was impossible and so the man, who had never prayed before, prayed with all his might: 'God, if you will make this bear a Christian I will be happy with whatever you want to do with me for the rest of my life.'

The bear was no more than three feet away from the man when it stopped dead in its tracks, looked up to the heavens quizzically, and then fell to its knees and prayed in a loud voice: 'Lord, bless this food which I am about to eat. Amen.'

Silly story, I know, but hopefully amusing nevertheless. It's easy to get confused about prayer. Believe me, you don't have to get down on your knees, close your eyes and speak earnestly in archaic language. Prayer is simply about building a relationship with God. I personally find it easiest to pray when I'm out driving, all by myself. Now that's a pretty difficult and rather dangerous thing to do while on your knees with both eyes closed.

God wants us to pray

Quite simply, prayer is conversation. And it's not just a one-way conversation. Christians believe that God hears us and loves to answer our prayers. The Bible says this: 'Ask and it will be given to you; seek and you will find; knock and the door will be opened for you. For everyone who asks receives; he who seeks finds; and to him who knocks the door will be opened' (Matthew 7:7–8).

God doesn't need us to pray so he can find out what we need from him. Jesus explained that God already knows what we need before we even utter a single word: 'Your Father knows what you need before you ask him' (Matthew 6:8). I believe God wants us to pray because it shows our reliance and dependence on him. Once again we come back to that word 'faith'. We ask him for things, or for help in impossible situations, believing that he'll hear our prayers, and our faith grows. 'Therefore I tell you, whatever you ask for in prayer, believe that you have received it, and it will be yours' (Mark 11:24). Jesus is saying to believe that you have received it. It's as simple as that.

There's another important reason we pray. It's so that we can build our relationship with our heavenly dad. He loves us and wants to get to know us, and he loves spending time with us. Prayer is about spending time with God.

The third reason God wants us to pray is so that we get involved with him in advancing the kingdom of God on earth.

When we consistently pray for opportunities to share the good news with our friends and neighbours and ask God for breakthrough, we work in partnership with God. It's brilliant.

Jesus' model

Like Bible study, prayer isn't something that becomes a cinch when you become a Christian. If we're really honest, we all find prayer hard from time to time, and it is certainly something we need to learn how to do. Let's see how Jesus encouraged his followers to pray:

> And when you pray, do not be like the hypocrites, for they love to pray standing in the synagogues and on the street corners to be seen by men. I tell you the truth, they have received their reward in full. But when you pray, go into your room, close the door and pray to your Father, who is unseen. Then your Father, who sees what is done in secret, will reward you. And when you pray, do not keep on babbling like pagans, for they think they will be heard because of their many words. Do not be like them, for your Father knows what you need before you ask him.
>
> This, then, is how you should pray:
>
> > Our Father in heaven,
> > hallowed be your name,
> > your kingdom come,
> > your will be done
> >   on earth as it is in heaven.
> > Give us today our daily bread.
> > Forgive us our debts,
> >   as we also have forgiven our debtors.
> > And lead us not into temptation,
> > but deliver us from the evil one.
>
> (Matthew 6:9–13)

I don't know if the Lord's Prayer sends a shiver down your spine as you recall your days in school. I know it takes me right back to school assemblies where a thousand of us stood and recited the prayer, parrot-fashion, after singing a rousing rendition of 'Fight the Good Fight' and hearing the results of the school football team. Jesus wasn't insisting that his disciples stuck rigidly to the exact words he spoke, but rather should use the prayer as a pattern for how they – and we – should pray. Let's break the prayer down and examine it a little closer.

1 'Our Father in heaven' – the prayer starts with God. A pretty good place to start. Right at the beginning it reminds us of our relationship with our heavenly dad. It starts by praising almighty God, who reigns in heaven but also wants to be our very best friend.

2 'Hallowed be your name' – so our prayers start with God, and now we move on to praising him. 'Hallowed' is another word for 'holy'. Our God is holy and perfect, and so different from us. Jesus encourages us to spend time reflecting on those aspects of God's amazing character.

3 'Your kingdom come, your will be done on earth as it is in heaven' – we can often come before God distracted by so many worries and distraction in our lives. Jesus encourages us to focus on what's really important – God's kingdom. It's not a case of resigning ourselves to pot luck in our lives, or that attitude of whatever will be, will be. We should pray that God's perfect plan and purposes be accomplished in our own lives but also in the world.

4 'Give us today our daily bread' – the prayer started with God, now it almost shifts a gear as it's asking God to meet our needs. And we're not just talking about a loaf of Hovis. Here we recognise that everything comes from God. He is our provider, and he knows what is best for us. I ask God to help me feed and clothe my family when I pray. I ask him to provide the money to pay the mortgage and the bills. I also

ask God to provide for others. Let's bring our practical needs before him, as he really is interested in every aspect of our lives.

5 'Forgive us our debts, as we also have forgiven our debtors' – let's face it, this is hard to do. If we've truly repented then Jesus has forgiven and forgotten our sin. But for us to forgive others – well, that often doesn't come quite so easy. When we pray let's not just try to forget the wrong and hurtful things that others have done to us, but let's try to forgive them, too.

6 'And lead us not into temptation, but deliver us from the evil one' – God doesn't tempt us and, indeed, temptation isn't sin. Even Jesus got tempted when he was in the wilderness for forty days and nights. Temptation is part and parcel of the fallen world that we all live in. We all get tempted, so let's ask God to help us overcome it.

There's no doubt about, the Lord's Prayer is a great framework for us to use in our prayers, so maybe consider using it to help you pray, but don't let it ever become a meaningless religious chant or monologue. Let me say it again, prayer is all about developing our relationship with God.

Persistence and patience

Our prayers show God that we are totally dependent on him. Jesus told his disciples a parable to show them that they should always pray and never give up:

'In a certain town there was a judge who neither feared God nor cared about men. And there was a widow in that town who kept coming to him with the plea, "Grant me justice against my adversary."

'For some time he refused. But finally he said to himself, "Even though I don't fear God or care about men, yet because this widow keeps bothering me, I will see that she gets justice, so that she won't eventually wear me out with her coming!" '

And the Lord said, 'Listen to what the unjust judge says. And will not God bring about justice for his chosen ones, who cry out to him day and night? Will he keep putting them off? I tell you, he will see that they get justice, and quickly. However, when the Son of Man comes, will he find faith on the earth?'

(Luke 18:1–8)

Jesus told the story to encourage his followers, who of course now include us, that God will listen to and honour persistent and patient prayer. The woman in the story repeatedly goes to a crooked judge with her pleas for justice and eventually wears him down so that he gives her what she asks for. Jesus contrasts this scenario with what we can expect when we make our requests to our heavenly dad. He says that God will give us justice – and pretty quick, too!

Effective prayer

We know that God wants to hear our prayers, and he gives us some guidelines that we need to take into consideration to make our prayer lives really effective. First, we need to pray according to God's will. There's a hilarious Arabian proverb that says, 'If God were to answer dogs' prayers, it would rain bones!' The well-known evangelist Billy Graham admitted, 'The only time my prayers aren't answered is on the golf course!' There's no doubt about it, God does answer prayers, though prayer isn't about twisting God's arm, hoping that he will give us what we want. Prayer is about relationship-building and discovering God's agenda, not ours. When we ask in this way, God responds.

But how do we know God's will? Well, as a friend of mine was forever saying, God's will is in his word. That's absolutely true. God's will is expressed throughout the Bible. That's another good reason why we should spend time reading the Bible, so we can know God's will. But, of course, there are situations in all of our lives where we don't know exactly what God's will is. The Scriptures don't specifically tell us whether we should go to university or whether we should get a job, whether we should get married or stay single . . . I think sometimes we need to put our hands up and admit we don't always know without a shadow of a doubt what God's will is in every single situation in our lives. We do know that God wants the best for us, so pray for a deeper understanding of which way to turn or what to do.

Let's always remember to pray with a sense of thanksgiving: 'Do not be anxious about anything, but in everything, by prayer and petition, with thanksgiving, present your requests to God' (Philippians 4:6). We all worry. We all have hard times and suffer times of great sadness. But we need to believe that God is in control. Paul was himself writing these words to the Christians in Philippi while imprisoned in Rome. His advice was to turn these worries into prayer that really works.

Fasting

It's worth mentioning fasting in this chapter, as to my mind it's an important part of our prayer life. Basically, fasting is going without food (not water) in order to get closer to God. Fasting helps us to pray and to see real breakthroughs or direction from God. Fasting is a discipline that Jesus kept and encouraged his disciples to keep:

> When you fast, do not look sombre as the hypocrites do, for they disfigure their faces to show men they are fasting. I tell you the truth, they have received their reward in full. But when you fast, put oil on your head and wash your face, so that it will not be obvious to men that you are

fasting, but only to your Father, who is unseen; and your Father, who sees what is done in secret, will reward you.

(Matthew 6:16–18)

Jesus expects us to fast but, like many aspects of our Christian lives, we're not to make a big 'show' of it and be a hypocrite. With regard to 'putting oil on your head' (v. 17), please don't panic here, as we need to look at the context in which it was said. In those days, olive oil was used like a normal cosmetic lotion that ordinary people would have worn every day as part of their usual day-to-day routine. So, in other words, Jesus was urging his followers to just go about their normal everyday business when they fasted so that others wouldn't know.

Like many disciplines, fasting is not easy, so if you've never done it before please don't start by attempting a forty-day fast – that would be plain daft. Instead, I'd encourage you to start with a one-day fast, from sunset to sunset. So you start after your evening meal on the Monday, for example, and fast until dinner on the Tuesday night. If you feel you can keep going then wait until after midnight or break your fast at breakfast the following morning. Fasting is going without food, but you must drink fluids, as going without water can seriously damage the kidneys.

In the Old Testament, Daniel fasted once for three weeks: 'At that time I, Daniel, mourned for three weeks. I ate no choice food; no meat or wine touched my lips; and I used no lotions at all until the three weeks were over' (Daniel 10:2–3). So with this three-week fast, Daniel abstained from delicacies like meat and wine, but would almost certainly have eaten bread and vegetables and drunk water. Now you may have a health condition like diabetes or anaemia that would make a complete fast dangerous, so why not do a fast like Daniel? Consider fasting other things instead: a chocolate fast, a coffee or tea fast, a TV fast. It's your heart attitude that matters, and when you fast, use that extra eating time instead with God, in prayer.

Creative prayer

Prayer isn't just for experts. It doesn't have to be a hard slog or boring, believe me. In September 1999, a bunch of young people just down the road from me on the south coast of England had the idea of trying to pray non-stop for a month. So that's what they did, and when God turned up they didn't stop until Christmas. From there the prayer meeting has spread into many nations, denominations and age groups. Hundreds of non-stop prayer meetings now link up on the Internet to form a unique chain of prayer across the globe.

Quite simply, '24–7' has become a world-wide, non-stop prayer movement. Participating groups pledge to pray twenty-four hours a day for a week or more in a dedicated prayer-room. They then 'carry the baton of prayer' for that period. The prayer passes from location to location in a never-ending flow linked up by the World-Wide Web. They are a virtual community praying in real locations. Right now someone, somewhere, is praying 24–7.

The 24–7 movement is a model that has proven unusually successful at mobilising people – especially young people – to pray as they've never prayed before. It might seem a silly thing to say, but people learned to pray by praying! And 24–7 has captured the imagination. The organisers have found that young people, for example, were more likely to turn up at a prayer meeting at 3 a.m. than at 7.30 p.m. because it's different, it's extreme. In fact, 24–7 makes prayer easier. Creativity plays an important part. Here are a few ideas that the 24–7 team use. See if they'll help to get you and your friends praying.

- Clothes peg prayer – create a wailing wall using chicken wire, clothes pegs and small pieces of paper. Write your prayer request on a piece of paper, clip it on to the chicken wire, and as you clip it on, pray for another one that is already hanging up.

- Birdseed prayer – have an area of wall covered in paper, have a bucket of birdseed and bucket of wallpaper paste and a brush. Use the wallpaper paste to paint the name of somebody you want to see become a Christian on the wall, and then throw birdseed at it as you pray. You will see that the more you throw bird seed on to the wall, the more seeds stick on the name of the person you are praying for.
- String of prayer – have lots of bits of string hanging from the ceiling. Staple on the bits of paper with your prayer requests. As you staple one up, pray for another.
- Post-it prayer – on a bit of wall use Post-it notes as prayer requests. Put one on the wall and pray for one that is already up.
- Chalk prayers – paint the prayer space completely black – floor, ceiling, walls – and as people come in and pray, get them to draw or write their prayers in white paint and chalk, so that eventually people's artwork and prayers completely cover the black space.
- International flavour – have maps, pictures from magazines and newspaper articles of different nations stuck on the walls, have a TV and video playing news recorded each day, or get videos from international charities like Tearfund, Cred or Christian Aid. Have these clips playing so people can pray for the situations as they see them unfold before their very eyes.
- Video – have a video of your town, shops or university, so people can pray as they see the images. Record the news and play it on video, or have BBC News 24 or Sky News on. Take a video camera out on to the streets and record interviews and images, and then have that playing for prayer.

Practical pointers

Please don't feel you're alone if you find prayer hard. We all feel like that from time to time. I do think it helps to recognise that most Christians find prayer difficult. I myself have been a

Christian for some twenty years and have read loads of books and heard hundreds of talks and sermons on prayer, yet still I struggle to get it right. I know it's vitally important to my walk with God, but there are always other things to do and pressures on my time. When I feel like that, I'm often reminded of the words of John Wesley: 'I'm so busy today that I really can't afford to spend less than two hours in prayer.' What a challenge that should be to all of us. Let me try to give you some really practical pointers to help you pray more often and more effectively:

1 *Pray with others*. I used to get together with my friend Allan every Wednesday morning at 7.00 a.m. for an hour before work. Allan used to get up because he knew I was coming and I had to drag my weary body out of bed because I knew he was waiting for me. We had some great times together. Praying with others is a good discipline.

2 *Make the time*. Communication isn't always easy, whether it be with another person or with God, so do make the time to do it consistently. Try to do it at least on a daily basis.

3 *Find a quiet place*. Our whole lives are made up of hustle and bustle, so find somewhere you can pray that is quiet and where you won't be disturbed. Turn off your phone. Put a 'do not disturb' sign on the door and spend some quality time with God.

4 *Focus and meditate on Jesus*. Try to escape the hurly-burly of twenty-first-century life for at least a few minutes. I'm not suggesting we empty our minds: instead, fill your mind with Jesus and how wonderful he is. It might help to play some Christian music at the same time to help focus your thoughts and prayers.

5 *Listen to God*. Don't let your prayers turn into a long shopping list. Be ready to listen to God as well as talk to him. Prayer is two-way communication, so don't do all the talking.

6 *Be flexible*. I'm reminded of a wonderful story that my good friend the well-known Christian speaker, broadcaster and

author Gerald Coates told of the time he was publicly challenged during a meeting. An irate church elder jumped to his feet and told Gerald what he thought about the absolute necessity for early-morning prayer. 'We need men in leadership positions who rise early each morning and spend an hour or more in prayer,' he bellowed from the audience halfway through Gerald's talk. Even Gerald was speechless for a few seconds, until the elder's wife stood up and asked her husband: 'If that's true, then why don't you do it?' If mornings aren't the best time for you, then don't feel you need to conform to other Christians' expectations of having an early-morning quiet time. Pray in the evening if it works better for you. Pray in your lunchtime. Pray on a long car journey. Pray when you're walking the dog. Just pray.

Prayer works

God can change things through prayer. James, an early church leader, encourages us to keep praying and not give up with these words: 'The prayer of a righteous man is powerful and effective. Elijah was a man just like us. He prayed earnestly that it would not rain, and it did not rain on the land for three and a half years! Again he prayed, and the heavens gave rain, and the earth produced its crops (James 5:16–18). Now that's pretty powerful praying.

As far as I'm concerned, I know that God has intervened in miraculous ways throughout my Christian life. I've personally witnessed healing through prayer so I know it works. I've seen God do little things and big things. At Christian events like Spring Harvest, for example, when working with hundreds of children I've seen God make verrucas and cold sores disappear before my very eyes. I've also seen God heal my daughter, Amber, who was rushed to hospital with a partly twisted bowel. God healed her and the surgery that had been recommended on the results of first set of X-rays was no longer needed. Even the surgeon was blown away when I informed him that God had healed little Amber. To say he was speechless would be a massive understatement. I'd really encourage you to keep a prayer diary, to write down your prayers as a kind of aide memoire, but also to record how God answered those very same prayers.

One of the most interesting characteristics of Jesus' and the disciples' praying is that when they prayed for others, they never finished their prayers by saying, 'If it be your will'. They were obviously so in touch with the Holy Spirit that they knew the will of God before they even opened their mouths in prayer. So when they encountered a specific situation that needed God's involvement, they immediately knew what should be done. Their praying was so positive that it often took the form of a direct command, and it was spoken with tremendous power and authority. Prayer was never meant to be boring or a religious repetitive ritual. Prayer is direct communication with a powerful God.

It's staggering, really, when you consider that the God of the entire universe is there to hear and help us. The brilliant scientist Sir Isaac Newton summed it up pretty well when he said that he could take his telescope and look millions and millions of miles into space. Then he added, 'But when I lay it aside, go into my room, shut the door, and get down on my knees in earnest prayer, I see more of Heaven and feel closer to the Lord than if I were assisted by all the telescopes on earth.' God is there for you, and in the words of a former British Telecom advertising campaign, remember, 'It's good to talk.'

Delving deeper

When should we pray?
1 Mark 1:35
2 Mark 14:38
3 Luke 3:21–2

4 Luke 6:12–13
5 James 5:13

Where should we pray?
1 Matthew 6:6
2 Matthew 18:19–20
3 Mark 1:35
4 Mark 6:46
5 Luke 5:16
6 Acts 1:14
7 Acts 2:42
8 Acts 12:12

What did Jesus teach about prayer?
1 Matthew 6:6
2 Matthew 6:9–13
3 Matthew 26:41
4 Luke 11:9
5 Luke 18:1–8
6 John 16:24

Memory verses

Therefore, since we have a great high priest who has gone through the heavens, Jesus the Son of God, let us hold firmly to the faith we profess. For we do not have a high priest who is unable to sympathise with our weaknesses, but we have one who has been tempted in every way, just as we are – yet was without sin. Let us then approach the throne of grace with confidence, so that we may receive mercy and find grace to help us in our time of need.

(Hebrews 4:14–16)

12

Evangelism

Evangelism is just one beggar telling another beggar where to find bread.

D.T. Niles

When something wonderful happens to you, you just can't help telling others. Good news is infectious. When my children were born I was telephoning family and friends with the news, even though it was near midnight and I got into trouble from the nurses for using my mobile phone on the ward. Good news is for sharing. It would have been wrong to have kept it to ourselves.

The story of Jesus is known as the 'gospel', which means 'good news'. That's what evangelism (a technical word that simply means 'telling others') is all about. It's a very natural process of telling people the good news of what has happened in your life. Don't worry if you're not good at talking or don't understand everything the Bible says, God wants to use you anyway. We do evangelism because it is such good news. It would be criminal to keep such wonderful news to ourselves. For the great Apostle Paul it was a privilege to share the gospel:

I am bound both to Greeks and non-Greeks, both to the wise and the foolish. That is why I am so eager to preach the gospel also to you who are at Rome.

I am not ashamed of the gospel, because it is the power of God for the salvation of everyone who believes: first for the Jew, then for the Gentile. For in the gospel a righteousness from God is revealed, a righteousness that is by faith from first to last, just as it is written: 'The righteous will live by faith.'

(Romans 1:14–17)

For us, sharing our faith shouldn't be seen as a chore or an effort. Never forget that it's good news we have to share, and good news is for sharing.

Jesus' strategy

God is a strategist. The entire Bible, from cover to cover, reflects God's strategy. From the very start of the Old Testament we see God's strategy worked out through men like Noah, Abraham, Joseph and David. They provided a backdrop for what was to come through Jesus. God had a plan, and his timing was perfect. Jesus came not just by accident – when God felt like it – but at a key moment in human history. Two thousand years ago, the Roman government was reasonably stable, the road system made travel more straightforward, and a common language, Greek, made communication easier.

In Matthew, we read of Jesus' strategy. 'Jesus went through all the towns and villages, teaching in their synagogues, preaching the good news of the kingdom and healing every disease and sickness' (Matthew 9:35). His strategy was to start in the small towns and villages, working his way towards Jerusalem. The well-known Jewish historian, Josephus, defines in his histories that Jesus' goal was to reach around 15,000 people in

204 villages. God had a specific strategy in mind and he put it into action through his beloved Son, Jesus, who came to save the world.

Before he returned to heaven, Jesus spoke one last time to his disciples, and he chose his final words very carefully. For him, evangelism was a major priority. These were his last words to his disciples before he ascended into heaven: 'But you will receive power when the Holy Spirit comes on you; and you will be my witnesses in Jerusalem, and in all Judea and Samaria, and to the ends of the earth' (Acts 1:8). Jesus here was sharing his fourfold vision and strategy for world-wide evangelisation. Let's take a closer look at the implications behind his final instructions.

Jerusalem – local
For the disciples Jerusalem was their local city, with a population of around 50,000. It was the place they lived and worked and also the place they had made the most mistakes. For us, too, this could well be the hardest place to evangelise. This is the place where people know you and know what you're really like! Your Jerusalem would probably include the place where you work, your immediate family and, of course, friends and neighbours.

Judea – national
Judea was the name of the large territory ruled by Herod the Great. It was the wider area outside Jerusalem. The culture and language would have been the same, but it was a bigger, arid, mountainous area. Our Judea is likely to be people that we see from time to time. Perhaps we only hear from them once or twice a year, at Christmas or around birthdays. These people may be colleagues from offices outside our immediate area that we know and have friendships with. Start thinking of neighbours who have moved away, or friends who have gone to universities in other parts of the country, or workmates who have been

transferred to other branches. Distant relatives could fall into this category.

If you start to jot names down you will probably end up with quite a list. How about putting this book down this very minute and giving them a call to say hello? Or write a note, or send an e-mail to maintain the contact and keep the relationship going. These are people you need to reach.

Samaria – cross-cultural

Samaria was built on a hill rising some 300 feet above the surrounding plain. In Jesus' day the Samaritans regarded themselves as part of Israel, but the Jews wanted nothing to do with the Samaritans, partly because it was the ancestors of the Samaritans who had opposed the rebuilding of Jerusalem. The Jews tried to avoid travelling through Samaria, and a Jew would not sit down to eat with a Samaritan. At times, Samaritans were regarded as worse and more ungodly than Gentiles.

Start to think about who you might choose not to talk to and spend time with, and this will be your Samaria. If you're the managing director of an international company then it could be the office cleaner, and vice versa. Then again, it might just be the down-and-out who sits at the bus stop drinking Special Brew from dawn to dusk. If you're still a student and in the sixth form at school, for example, the kids in the first year, who you just refuse to even acknowledge, might be your Samaria. For me, it was my neighbour, June, who I once called a 'stupid woman' (I know, it's terrible, isn't it) and then felt I had to apologise to and buy a small gift. Going to Samaria will make other people sit up and take notice, because it's not normal – so go and do it.

Ends of the earth – international

The ends of the earth have no limits whatsoever. With the opportunities in world travel, I guess there's probably not one single country on earth that you couldn't be in within around thirty-six hours. One of the highlights of my years of ministry was preaching the gospel at a squatter camp in one of the most dangerous cities in the world, Johannesburg. In the midst of incredible squalor, with yours truly standing on the back of an old pickup truck, sharing the gospel with a sea of haunted and poverty-stricken black faces, I was reminded of the words of the great missionary C.T. Studd: 'Some wish to live within the sound of church and chapel bell. I wish to run a rescue mission within a yard of hell.' That day, amid the poverty and violence, large numbers of men, women, boys and girls met the Lord Jesus for themselves. It was awesome.

There's something about going to other countries and cultures that stirs faith and makes you change for good. Before his untimely death in a tragic plane accident in July 1982, American musician and evangelist Keith Green would challenge people by asking: 'We should not be asking ourselves the question "Should we go?" The question is, "Is God telling me to stay?" ' If it's just impossible for you to go right now, why not invest money in others who are able? How about adopting a missionary and investing money into their ministry – your regular support could make all the difference.

David Livingstone once wrote in his journal about his 'selfless' missionary life:

People talk of the sacrifice I have made in spending so much of my life in Africa. Can that be called a sacrifice which is simply paying back a small part of the great debt owing to our God, which we can never repay? Is that a sacrifice which brings its own blest reward in healthful activity, the consciousness of doing good, peace of mind and a bright hope of glorious destiny hereafter? Away with the word in such a view and with such a thought! It is emphatically no sacrifice. Say rather it is a privilege.

Sharing your faith is a privilege. Don't panic or feel out of your depth if you don't know everything about Jesus, God and the Bible. You also don't have to get a sensible suit, a serious haircut and a big black Bible to bash your friends over the head with, or grow a beard. Just tell them of the wonderful change in your life, and tell it as it really is.

Making friends – evangelism the easy way

There's so much I could say about evangelism. I suppose I could recommend my book, *The A–Z of Evangelism* (published by Hodder and Stoughton, 2002), but modesty prevents me doing so. We could talk here about many different aspects of how to share our faith, but to my mind it makes sense to look at the most effective and probably the most fun way – through friendship and relationships.

As well as being great fun, friendships and relationships are vitally important to God. In the beginning, in Eden, when God created the world – and, in it, humankind – there was still something that was not quite right. There was something missing. God and Adam were not enough. Adam needed friendship with other human beings, so God created Eve, the missing piece of the puzzle. Quite simply, humankind was made for friendship and relationships.

Friendship evangelism is also the most effective form of evangelism. A major survey was taken in the early 1980s when 10,000 people were asked the question: 'What was responsible for you coming to Christ and this church?' The results made for very interesting reading:

Evangelistic crusades	½%
Organised visitation	1%
Special need	2%
Just walked in	3%
Special event	3%

Sunday School	3%
Pastoral contact	6%
Friend or relative	79%

(Source: The Institute of Church Growth, Pasadena, California)

Although it's been twenty years or so since those original statistics were formulated, the Church Growth Institute have formulated similar figures with groups in hundreds of seminars, and the numbers still hold true today:

Advertisement	2%
Organised visitation	6%
Pastoral contact	6%
Friend or relative	86%

These figures should have tremendous implications for all Christians. They show clearly that friendships and relationships appear to be the best way of reaching the lost. If we want to change the world we must live in the world. To the men reading this who are desperate to reach their mates at the pub on a Sunday night, you're not going to do it by sitting at home drinking cocoa and watching *Songs of Praise*. We must get out of our cosy Christian lives and start making an effort to make friends and begin being Good News.

Funny, isn't it – when it comes to evangelism most of us try the difficult things first: door-to-door work, stopping people in the street to give them a gospel tract, or singing cheesy Christian folk songs outside Sainsbury's and getting in everyone's way on a busy Saturday afternoon. A few knock-backs or bad experiences can be pretty soul-destroying and can sometimes put Christians off doing evangelism altogether. However, inviting your neighbours around, or taking them out for a drink, or going to see a movie with them, is a different matter altogether and can bring a completely different response. You might actually enjoy it and want to do it again, so that can't be bad, can it? Here are some of my top tips on how to be a better friend.

Quality time

You get to know someone by spending time with them, so first and foremost choose to invest quality time with your friends. I'll be perhaps a tad controversial here and suggest you shouldn't get so wrapped up in church activities that you don't have the time to spend with your old friends who aren't yet Christians. Include them and don't forget them.

For me, that means prioritising an evening a week for a boys' night at our local Sports and Social Club. Every Sunday, almost without fail, from 9 p.m. you'll find us enjoying a few pints, having a laugh and talking about everything under the sun. Then, in the week, if there seems to be a good football match in prospect, the lads will come round to my home and we'll watch the game together. At other times, we get together with our wives for a meal, and often we'll do something all together with our children: a walk in the country, a barbecue or swimming or flying kites down on the beach. We even went on holiday with our neighbours – sharing a caravan for good measure. It was a blast.

Prayer

Prayer is the secret ingredient in evangelism. Martin Luther said, 'As it is the business of tailors to make clothes and of cobblers to mend shoes, so it is the business of Christians to pray.' Our prayers make all the difference, so let's be specific and focused.

For our neighbours Scott and Martine, there have been at least three occasions where God has intervened in quite dramatic ways. Martine encountered problems during pregnancy, then when baby Louis was finally born his arm was dislocated and the nerves in his arm were badly damaged. Third, we prayed for the healing of their niece, who was critically injured in a horrendous road accident. Her condition seemed so desperate, she was even administered the 'last rites'.

God stepped into each of these situations in remarkable ways. Martine gave birth safely, a paediatric consultant has said Louis's arm is perfect and he no longer needs any physiotherapy or other treatment, and their niece is home from hospital and making a remarkable recovery. Isn't God good!

Introduce them to your Christian friends

It's important to choose the right ones here. During a boys' night out at our local curry house when we were celebrating my birthday, one of my Christian friends asked my mate Bruno what he thought about judgment and eternal damnation. Definitely not the most sensitive thing to ask on a low-key night out while enjoying a glass of wine and a chicken vindaloo. Poor old Bruno almost choked on his chapatti.

I'm absolutely convinced that half the battle here is showing unbelievers that Christians aren't all wallys in flares, sandals and beards – and that's just the women! Joking aside, let's show them we're ordinary people who have met God in an extraordinary way.

Tell your story

Your own personal story of how you met Jesus can be incredibly effective. When you've earned the right to do so, start to share your experiences of how God helps you through life, and how you met him for yourself. Done quite naturally, this will be very normal and could have a profound effect. You may not know the Bible inside out and may have problems answering tough questions about your new-found faith, but no one can question your own story of how you found Jesus.

A missionary in India was once teaching the Bible to a group of Hindu ladies. Halfway through the lesson, one of the women got up and walked out. A short time later, she came back and listened more intently than ever. At the close of the hour the leader enquired, 'Why did you leave the meeting? Weren't you interested?'

'Oh yes,' the Hindu lady replied. 'I was so impressed with what you had to say about Christ that I went out to ask your driver whether you really lived the way you talked. When he said you did, I hurried back so I wouldn't miss out on anything.'

Your story and life will speak volumes.

Invite them to events

Once again, think about this carefully. Unfortunately, your average Sunday meeting might not be the best thing to invite your friend to. So it might be better to wait for the monthly guest meeting, where things are especially geared for outsiders. Christmas and Easter are times that more people go to church, so that might be more appropriate. If that's still not suitable, something less threatening, like a meal or other social event, could be just the occasion for your friend to meet more Christians, enjoy themselves and hear more about Christianity.

What do they need from you?

Have a good think about what your friends might need from you. By that I mean it could be emotional support or they might need more practical help. Maybe it's an elderly neighbour you could cook for, or just visit or invite in for a chat and a cup of tea. A while ago, a new couple moved into our street, so we bought them a bottle of wine and a card which my wife took over. They were absolutely bowled over as no one had ever done anything like that before.

The women in our church are great when it comes to another mum, be they part of our church or not, giving birth. Someone straight away draws up a rota, and that family is delivered a good hot meal for at least a week. You wouldn't believe the impact that can have on the rest of the neighbourhood when they see a steady stream of meals arriving every night at teatime. Once again, it gives us a very natural and normal reason to explain our motivation for doing it.

Listen to them

Two men were talking one day. One of them said, 'My wife talks to herself a lot.'

His friend answered, 'Mine does, too, but she doesn't know it. She thinks I'm listening.'

Communication is a vital form of building a good friendship, though once again bear in mind the profound words of the Greek philosopher Diogenes: 'We have two ears and one mouth that we may listen the more and talk the less.'

Listen to your friends and don't talk about yourself all the time – it can be so irritating. It drives me up the wall, and I tend to call it the 'taxi driver mentality'. Apologies to all taxi drivers out there who aren't like this, but most of the ones I've encountered are the kind of people who, if you've got a black cat, then they'll own a panther called Shadow. They tend to be the world's biggest experts on everything. Do you know the sort of people I mean? No one likes a know-it-all, so don't talk about yourself all the time. Don't even talk about the Lord all the time (I'm sure he won't mind). Don't come up with all the right answers. Trust me, your friends won't appreciate it. Instead, listen to them and think about how Jesus can help them.

Be honest about yourself

While thinking about this point I was reminded of a story of a minister who was trying to say in his Sunday sermon that none of us is perfect, and not only that, none of us today even has the opportunity of knowing a perfect person. In fact, he went so far as to challenge the people, asking them if any of them had even heard of a perfect person. He was understandably surprised when one man actually stood up and stated that he knew of such a person. The dumbfounded vicar asked him for details. Did he really know him? Had he met him? The man admitted that he didn't know the man personally, but he had certainly heard a great deal about him. In fact, this legendary man of many perfections was his wife's first husband.

None of us are perfect, so let's be honest about our failures and confide, where appropriate, in our friends. But let's also share our dreams and aspirations as well as enjoying telling them how God has answered our prayers.

Be patient

They do say that the average person, if there is such a thing, has to hear the gospel seven times before they make a decision to follow Christ. So be patient. A little tip here: it's sometimes easier to have patience with others when we remember God's patience towards us, so remember that when you get particularly impatient and frustrated.

Some years ago, Dr James Engel, a marketing professor at Ohio State University, developed a scale which looks at the process a person goes through on the road to knowing Jesus and becoming a disciple. Now I know what you're thinking – God doesn't have to work to scales or diagrams. Absolutely true. But this scale might be helpful in seeing how the Good News can work, and where your friend might be on their journey to faith in Christ.

-8 Awareness of Supreme Being
-7 Initial awareness of the gospel
-6 Awareness of the fundamentals of the gospel
-5 A grasp of the implications of the gospel
-4 Positive attitude towards the gospel
-3 A recognition of personal problems
-2 Decision to do something about it
-1 Repentance and new faith in Jesus
    NEW CREATION
+1 Evaluation of decision
+2 Integration into the Church

+3 Conceptual and behavioural growth
+4 Communion with God
+5 Active in evangelism

Bear this journey in mind when you're feeling impatient. Remember the Dutch proverb: 'A handful of patience is worth more than a bushel of brains.' Keep going and keep praying and ask God for breakthrough.

Enjoy it

The problem with producing lists is that some people think they're some sort of magic formula. Friendship isn't a formula, it's a natural process that should be great fun. Over the years I've spent a lot of time with friends, eating at my local Indian restaurant and in time getting to know the staff and management as well – indeed, so well that I now count them as friends. When Jemma, my wife, and I got married, we invited a contingent from Tandoori Nights to join us and celebrate our big day with us.

I've got to say I was dead chuffed to see the manager, Mr Miah, and his family turn up, and was intrigued by the two huge presents he struggled through the doors with. It was the first Christian meeting they'd ever been to and they loved it. As a mark of their friendship they had bought us a barbecue and a microwave oven. We were so touched. Seven years later, Mr Miah and the gang at Tandoori Nights aren't saved, but I firmly believe they're all a little further down the road to knowing more about Jesus, and that's the very nature of what friendship evangelism is all about – making friends and bringing people closer to Jesus.

I get misunderstood and criticised by people in the church I go to for having a few pints, but I don't care one bit. I've already mentioned our boys' get-togethers on Sundays – well, we baptised our first two members a while ago. Isn't that fantastic? Our neighbours Scott and Martine have become two of our closest friends, and their son classes my wife, our children and me as part of his family. Christian friends are wonderful and very important, but just think of all the other friends you could have if you looked out of church and instead looked at those around you. You too could probably have wonderful neighbours like ours.

Let's finish this chapter with one last quote, this time from Indian yogi Paramahansa Yogananda: 'There is a magnet in your heart that will attract true friends. That magnet is unselfishness, thinking of others first . . . when you learn to live for others, they will live for you.'

Delving deeper

Why did Jesus evangelise?
1 Mark 6:34
2 Luke 19:10
3 John 10:10
4 2 Peter 3:9
5 1 Timothy 2:3–6

How is the gospel described?
1 Ephesians 1:13
2 Ephesians 3:6
3 Ephesians 6:15
4 Colossians 1:23
5 2 Timothy 2:8

How did the early Church do evangelism?
1 Luke 9:6
2 Acts 3:6
3 Acts 4:20
4 Acts 9:27
5 1 Corinthians 2:3–5
6 2 Corinthians 5:18
7 Colossians 4:2–6

Memory verses

But even if you should suffer for what is right, you are blessed. 'Do not fear what they fear; do not be frightened.' But in your hearts set apart Christ as Lord. Always be prepared to give an answer to everyone who asks you to give the reason for the hope that you have. But do this with gentleness and respect.

(1 Peter 3:14–15)

13

Communion

> The bread and wine of Communion are visible, tangible emblems of Christ's body given and blood shed on the cross for our sins.
>
> *John R. W. Stott*

The Lord's Supper, Communion (because we commune with God and other Christians) or Eucharist (thanksgiving) are different names for the other sacrament that Jesus asked that his followers keep. Readers who have followed my text faithfully and logically thus far may remember that the other sacrament to be followed was baptism. Of course, baptism only happens once, but Communion is to be taken throughout our Christian lives as a simple sign of our love for Jesus.

Jesus instituted the first Communion the night before he was due to die, and it happened in the context of a meal with his very best friends. The actual meal was the Passover meal – an annual meal to remember and celebrate delivery of the Jewish people from slavery in Egypt. Similarly, the Lord's Supper began to celebrate the deliverance from our sin because of Jesus' death. Take a look at what happened:

> While they were eating, Jesus took bread, gave thanks and broke it, and gave it to his disciples, saying, 'Take and eat; this is my body.' Then he took the cup, gave thanks and offered it to them, saying, 'Drink from it, all of you. This is my blood of the covenant, which is poured out for many for the forgiveness of sins. I tell you, I will not drink of this fruit of the vine from now on until that day when I drink it anew with you in my Father's kingdom.'
>
> (Matthew 26:26–9)

The story is also told in Mark 14:12–25, Luke 22:7–38 and John 13–14. Paul also spoke about Communion:

> For I received from the Lord what I also passed on to you: The Lord Jesus, on the night he was betrayed, took bread, and when he had given thanks, he broke it and said, 'This is my body, which is for you; do this in remembrance of me.' In the same way, after supper he took the cup, saying, 'This cup is the new covenant in my blood; do this, whenever you drink it, in remembrance of me.' For whenever you eat this bread and drink this cup, you proclaim the Lord's death until he comes.
>
> (1 Corinthians 11:23–6)

Significance and symbolism

Christians have been celebrating Communion for some 2,000 years and it has a great deal of significance and symbolism, as the 'meal' is shared with other believers.

Remembrance

Jesus himself said, 'Do this in remembrance of me.' When we take Communion we remember his death, and the bread and wine create a vivid picture. The bread represents his body, beaten up and broken. Then the wine represents the blood shed as he died on the cross to take the punishment our sins deserved.

Proclamation

It was Paul who reminded us that every time we share Communion it's a proclamation: 'For whenever you eat this bread and drink this cup, you proclaim the Lord's death until he comes' (1 Corinthians 11:26). I guess it's easy to take things for granted if Communion becomes a religious ritual. Paul encourages us here to think about what Jesus went through because of his incredible love for us.

Nourishment

Just as meat and two veg or a good curry physically nourishes our bodies, so eating the bread and drinking the wine gives us spiritual nourishment. Jesus said:

> I tell you the truth, unless you eat the flesh of the Son of Man and drink his blood, you have no life in you. Whoever eats my flesh and drinks my blood has eternal life, and I will raise him up at the last day. For my flesh is real food and my blood is real drink. Whoever eats my flesh and drinks my blood remains in me, and I in him. Just as the living Father sent me and I live because of the Father, so the one who feeds on me will live because of me.
>
> (John 6:53–7)

Now, clearly, Jesus wasn't talking about cannibalism here. He certainly wasn't speaking literally to his friends. Instead, he had in mind a spiritual eating and drinking through our sharing in Communion.

Fellowship

Communion is a time when we 'commune' with other Christians as well as God. It's a sign of our unity with other believers.

In fact, Paul said: 'Because there is one loaf, we, who are many, are one body, for we all partake of the one loaf' (1 Corinthians 10:17). I think that speaks for itself.

Participation

There are different denominational views of who should take Communion and how, but most would agree that only true believers of Jesus should take the bread and wine. After all, as we've already seen, Communion is a sign of being a Christian and following the Christian way of life. Because of this, I think age in a sense is immaterial and I think it's fantastic when children are able to share Communion along with adults. The key is whether they love Jesus, not how long they've been a Christian or the size of their Bible.

The Apostle Paul went so far as to warn of the dangers of taking Communion if a person isn't right with God. He explained that serious consequences would follow: 'For anyone who eats and drinks without recognising the body of the Lord eats and drinks judgment on himself. That is why many among you are weak and sick, and a number of you have fallen asleep' (1 Corinthians 11:29–30). That really is serious stuff. Let's always remember to re-examine ourselves before we take Communion and be right with God, our heavenly dad.

As to how often Communion should be celebrated, the Bible is silent. Some churches celebrate Communion every week. At my friend's church in Northern Ireland, it is in their constitution to celebrate it every week without fail. Other churches will take it once a month, or even once a quarter. Paul simply said, 'For whenever you eat this bread and drink this cup, you proclaim the Lord's death until he comes' (1 Corinthians 11:26). So, in one sense, 'whenever' means 'whenever'! It certainly doesn't have to be on a Sunday to make it more special.

The Bible is also silent on who should actually lead the thing through and who should actually administer the bread and wine. It makes sense for a vicar, minister or leader to do it, but nowhere do the Scriptures tell us that this is the way it should be done. You may wish to celebrate Communion after a meal with your family, or in the context of a house group. The key is not what rank or position we hold in the church, but whether we love Jesus or not.

Delving deeper

Why do we take Communion?
1 Matthew 26:26
2 John 6:53–7
3 1 Corinthians 10:17
4 1 Corinthians 11:26

Who should take Communion?
1 1 Corinthians 11:27–9
2 1 Corinthians 11:29–30

How did Jesus celebrate Communion?
1 Matthew 26:20–30
2 Mark 14:17–26
3 Luke 22:14–30
4 John 13:21–30

Memory verses

> For I received from the Lord what I also passed on to you:
> The Lord Jesus, on the night he was betrayed, took bread,
> and when he had given thanks, he broke it and said, 'This
> is my body, which is for you; do this in remembrance of
> me.' In the same way, after supper he took the cup, saying,
> 'This cup is the new covenant in my blood; do this,
> whenever you drink it, in remembrance of me.' For when-
> ever you eat this bread and drink this cup, you proclaim
> the Lord's death until he comes.
>
> (1 Corinthians 11:23–6)

14

Money

Building one's life on a foundation of gold is just like building a house on foundations of sand.

Henrik Ibsen

When she was a little girl, Woolworth heiress Barbara Hutton's favourite game was make-believe. She wanted to become a princess and she wanted to be loved for who she was, and not for what she had. In her lifetime she married seven times, each time searching for the perfect man to fulfil her dreams, her handsome prince in shining armour. In the end, despite her staggering wealth, she was just a vulnerable, sick, lonely old woman. 'I inherited everything but love,' she told her biographer, Philip Van Rensselaer. 'I've always been searching for it, because I didn't know what it was.'

J. Paul Getty, who died in June 1976, was widely acclaimed as one of the world's richest men, yet was impoverished in almost every way apart from his vast fortunes. He married five times, and every marriage ended in divorce. His four older sons were terrified of him, and his youngest, who died aged only twelve, hardly knew him. Money was a curse for him. It distorted everything he did.

Billionaire Howard Hughes made his fortune from his TWA airline, Las Vegas hotels and Hollywood films, yet died – a recluse – of malnutrition. His pitiful belongings filled one suitcase and at his funeral his relatives had to club together to buy him a suit to be buried in. It was almost impossible to believe he had once been one of the richest men ever in America.

Money is a funny thing. Some people live for it. Some people die for it. Can anyone out there lend me a fiver? Jesus talked a great deal about money and the problems it caused people. In fact, one-fifth of all Jesus had to say was about money. Sixteen of the thirty-eight parables in the Old Testament were concerned with how to handle money and possessions. Later on in the Gospels, an amazing one out of ten verses (288 in all) deal directly with the subject of money. The Bible has 500 verses on prayer, fewer than 500 verses on faith, but more than 2,350 verses on money and possessions. During a time of teaching one day, Jesus said this to his disciples:

Do not store up for yourselves treasures on earth, where moth and rust destroy, and where thieves break in and steal. But store up for yourselves treasures in heaven, where moth and rust do not destroy, and where thieves do not break in and steal. For where your treasure is, there your heart will be also.

The eye is the lamp of the body. If your eyes are good, your whole body will be full of light. But if your eyes are bad, your whole body will be full of darkness. If then the light within you is darkness, how great is that darkness!

No one can serve two masters. Either he will hate the one and love the other, or he will be devoted to the one and despise the other. You cannot serve both God and Money.

(Matthew 6:19–24)

Clearly the subject of money is an important one. We do live in a very materialistic society, and it's all too easy to get caught up in the value system of the world and be always trying to keep up with the Joneses or whoever happens to live next door to you. So many people you and I know spend their lives storing up money and possessions, only to die and leave them all behind. Jesus was calling his disciples, who of course now include us, to be happy and contented with what we have and never to let our money and possessions 'possess' us.

Money matters

Contrary to popular misquotation the Bible never said, 'Money is the root of all evil.' Look at what was actually said:

> But godliness with contentment is great gain. For we brought nothing into the world, and we can take nothing out of it. But if we have food and clothing, we will be content with that. People who want to get rich fall into temptation and a trap and into many foolish and harmful desires that plunge men into ruin and destruction. For the love of money is a root of all kinds of evil. Some people, eager for money, have wandered from the faith and pierced themselves with many griefs.
>
> (1 Timothy 6:6–10)

This sage advice from Paul was given to Timothy, a young church leader and one of his closest companions. Look again at verse 10: 'For the love of money is a root of all kinds of evil.' Money isn't evil in itself. Open your wallet for a moment and remove a banknote. After the moths have flown away and the Queen's eyes have become accustomed to the daylight, look at what you see. What's evil about that piece of paper sitting on your hand? Absolutely nothing. After all, it's hardly likely to bash you on the head, now is it? It's the 'love' of money that is the key to the issue. I wonder how much you or I love money.

And how far would you go to get more of it?

Tony Marlow of New York City made the papers some years ago when someone offered him $2,000 to run naked through the streets for five minutes. He took up the challenge and the money just about paid his bail. Another time, another American citizen, Christopher Brent of Philadelphia, was bet by a 'friend' that he wouldn't jump out of an eighth-floor window. The reward? Just $800. Brent did it, but he didn't collect.

Both of these stories are absolutely true.

Both of these men were desperate for more money. They loved money and that's the very thing that Paul was warning against. We can also draw some other valuable (if you'll excuse the pun) lessons from Paul's first letter to Timothy.

1 We need to realise that one day all we own will be gone (v. 7).
2 There's a big difference between needs and wants. Personally, I'd love a bigger house with a huge garden, spa bath, sauna, swimming pool and a snooker room, but I don't need it. Paul was content with what he had and he encourages us to be content with what we've got (v. 8).
3 We must always watch our motives for wanting and getting more (v. 9).
4 Greed can have serious consequences and will lead to 'ruin and destruction' (v. 9).
5 Love God more than money. He has to be our first love (v. 11).

Old Testament giving

In the Old Testament, the Israelites gave a 'tithe' (a tenth) of their income for the support of the Levites (who were nothing to do with jeans, I might add), their spiritual leaders of the day. These funds freed up these men to teach and preach to people about God without having to worry about earning money to pay the bills. But tithing was in use long before the days of Moses. Right from the beginning, great men of God like Abraham and Jacob tithed:

'And blessed be God Most High,
who delivered your enemies into your hand.'
Then Abram gave him a tenth of everything.

(Genesis 14:20)

This stone that I have set up as a pillar will be God's house, and of all that you give me I will give you a tenth.

(Genesis 28:22)

Three tithes are mentioned in the Old Testament: the Levitical tithe, which I've already mentioned, a Festival tithe and, every three years, a tithe for the poor and destitute.

New Testament giving

The New Testament doesn't command tithing specifically, though I do believe that everyone who earns money should tithe. Jesus does commend tithing, though, in a fiery encounter with a bunch of religious hypocrites: 'Woe to you, teachers of the law and Pharisees, you hypocrites! You give a tenth of your spices – mint, dill and cumin. But you have neglected the more important matters of the law – justice, mercy and faithfulness. You should have practised the latter, without neglecting the former' (Matthew 23:23). For these hypocrites, giving wasn't about the amount they gave, but how they gave it and how much they kept back for themselves. It's the same for us today. God looks beyond the number of noughts on the cheque and looks at our hearts.

We can learn a lot from the early Church. They were certainly far from stingy: 'For I testify that they gave as much as they were able, and even beyond their ability' (2 Corinthians 8:3). Paul had been collecting money for the Christians in Jerusalem who had absolutely nothing. The churches in Macedonia gave generously even though they were poor. They had given considerably more than even Paul could have hoped for as they sacrificially gave to help their brothers and sisters in Christ. Wouldn't it be an honour if people said that about you or me?

Giving generously

Martin Luther astutely observed, 'There are three conversions necessary: the conversion of the heart, the mind and the purse.' Of these three, it may well be that many of us find the conversion of the purse the most difficult. So let's examine some other verses about giving.

Freely and cheerfully

God's not going to send the boys round if you don't pay him what he deserves. He's not the proprietor of some dodgy East-End debt collecting agency – he's your heavenly dad. 'Each man should give what he has decided in his heart to give, not reluctantly or under compulsion, for God loves a cheerful giver' (2 Corinthians 9:7). It seems to me that it's not so much 'what' we give, but 'how' we give. If you can't give happily and cheerfully, then keep your money in your pocket.

Regularly and systematically

Paul was here offering some very practical advice for the early Church that still holds true to this day: 'On the first day of every week, each one of you should set aside a sum of money in keeping with his income, saving it up, so that when I come no collections will have to be made' (1 Corinthians 16:2). It's a good discipline to seriously think about what you're going to give away and do it consistently, rather than just giving whatever happens to be left in your pocket. I personally know from my own ministry, which is funded mainly from gifts, how useful it is to know what is likely to come in each month. Really down-to-earth and boring things like standing orders make life easier for the beneficiaries of your giving.

In secret
Don't give so everyone can see how generous you are. Once again, that's a wrong motive:

> Be careful not to do your 'acts of righteousness' before men, to be seen by them. If you do, you will have no reward from your Father in heaven.
> So when you give to the needy, do not announce it with trumpets, as the hypocrites do in the synagogues and on the streets, to be honoured by men. I tell you the truth, they have received their reward in full. But when you give to the needy, do not let your left hand know what your right hand is doing, that your giving may be in secret. Then your Father, who sees what is done in secret, will reward you.
>
> (Matthew 6:1–4)

I know, if I'm honest, in the past I've given gifts with mixed motives either because I might get something back in return or because I secretly want others to see how generous I am. I have to confess to once putting an anonymous cash gift through someone's door, then deliberately taking a very slow walk down their garden path to the gate, then a slow dawdle past their house in the hope that they might have seen me. Once again, that is well out of order and is hypocrisy. Even though the actions were good, the motives were all wrong. That's why Paul says it is so good to do these things 'in secret'.

Sowing and reaping
Jesus here uses an interesting metaphor taken from measuring grain so as to ensure that the full volume is given: 'Give, and it

will be given to you. A good measure, pressed down, shaken together and running over, will be poured into your lap. For with the measure you use, it will be measured to you' (Luke 6:38). Jesus is saying that we get back what we put in, but much more besides when we give to God.

Money management

I wonder if you're managing your money, or whether money is managing you? It's a tricky question to answer. Given that money is the second most talked-about subject in the Bible, it's an issue we seriously need to think about.

Debt is a serious issue. In the UK since January 1996, 156,905 homes have been repossessed. Homeowners owe at least £963m in mortgage arrears. Realistically this figure is probably an understatement because it doesn't include arrears amounting to less than three months' repayments. Nor does it include interest claimed by lenders on repossession shortfalls. Around one in 250 mortgages still ends in repossession.

Debt and credit cards pose difficult problems. We all live in a society where we always want bigger and better. Many of us buy things we don't really need with money we don't really have, to impress people we don't really like. This very morning I went shopping to buy a shirt. There were a number of reductions which I thought were just too good to miss, so I picked them up too and dumped them all on the cashier's counter. The cashier told me that if I signed up for a store credit card I'd get an additional 10 per cent off and £500 to spend there and then. I never particularly wanted a Burton's store card but, I thought to myself, what harm could it do? And with that extra 10 per cent they're practically giving the stuff away, so I'd better get some more clothes. Now I didn't succumb to the temptation, left the application form unsigned and went home with what I'd wanted – but it would have been so easy.

There are thousands of people in serious debt, and I can put my hands up and admit that I was one of them. Large debt had a crippling effect on me some five years ago. For a period of time I was using one credit card to pay off the minimum repayment on another. It was a ridiculous situation. Credit cards are so easy for all of us to obtain, and at one stage I had ten platinum cards, with enough credit to buy a small house. I came to a point where I realised I was in trouble and got help. I cut them all up and worked out a way of repaying my debts that was possible for me and acceptable to the credit card companies. My credit cards were causing me to stumble, so I got rid of them. These days I only use debit cards, which means I can only buy what I can afford. Maybe that's something you should consider doing for yourself. That way, I feel personally, is more honouring to God.

Our giving

God doesn't need our money. But you and I need the wonderful experience of giving it. Of course, we need to always remember that we are saved because of the amazing grace of God. Keeping the Ten Commandments and tithing won't buy anyone a ticket to heaven. However, Jesus said: 'For where your treasure is, there your heart will be also' (Matthew 6:21). So where is your treasure?

You may choose to give a tenth of your gross income to the local church and then extra giving on top. You might choose to 'adopt' a worker in some far-flung corner of the world, or a full-time Christian in your home town, by setting up a standing order to give to them regularly to partner in their ministry. For far too long, ministers, evangelists, youth workers and, in particular, missionaries have been expected to live on peanuts, while the majority of their fellow church members are doing very nicely.

There's no doubt about it, to extend the kingdom of God money is needed. Those who work full-time in Christian work need to be paid, as do missionaries serving God in different and sometimes very difficult situations all across the world. The local church should also be helping the poor and those in genuine financial difficulties, as well as paying for more mundane things like the heating and maintenance of buildings. Whatever you choose to do, do it freely and cheerfully (don't forget what it says in 2 Corinthians 9:7). So don't be mean. As Paul reminds us again and again, the only way to give is to give out of love. Giving shouldn't be a pain. It should be a pleasure.

Delving deeper

Look at some examples of tithing in the Old Testament
1 Leviticus 27:30–3
2 Numbers 18:20–32
3 Deuteronomy 12:5–19
4 Deuteronomy 14:22–7

What problems can money cause?
1 Luke 15:29–31
2 Matthew 19:16–18
3 Luke 8:14
4 Luke 12:22–4
5 Luke 16:1–9

How should we help the poor?
1 Acts 4:34–5
2 2 Corinthians 8:3
3 2 Corinthians 8:13–14
4 James 2:14–17

How should Christians give?
1 Matthew 6:1–4
2 Luke 6:38
3 1 Corinthians 16:2
4 2 Corinthians 9:6–11

Memory verses

Whoever can be trusted with very little can also be trusted with much, and whoever is dishonest with very little will also be dishonest with much. So if you have not been trustworthy in handling worldly wealth, who will trust you with true riches?

(Luke 16:10–11)

15

The Return of Jesus

The primitive church thought more about the Second Coming of Jesus Christ than about death or about heaven. The early Christians were looking not for a cleft in the ground called a grave but for a cleavage in the sky called Glory. They were watching not for the undertaker but for the uppertaker.

Alexander Maclaren

I wandered into a Christian bookshop in Bournemouth one day, and while browsing through the mountain of books got into a conversation with the shop manageress. The lovely lady was very interested in what I did, and when I explained that I was an escapologist her eyes lit up. 'Oooh,' she enthused, 'I feel the Lord is drawing me into escapology too. I've always been fascinated by the end times.'

I just about managed to suppress my laughter at the image conjured up in my mind of this rather plump, Hattie Jacques lookalike, manacled by her ankles and dangling precariously from a crane while trying to extricate herself from a straitjacket! For far from being interested in escapology, she was into 'eschatology', which means a study of the 'last things'. In other words, what will happen in the future, at the end of time.

As human beings, we don't know what is going to happen – or, for that matter, when. If we did know everything, we'd be the same as God, who, as we've seen, is all-knowing. Throughout the pages of the Bible God has told us about important events that will be happening in the future, and a vital thread running throughout is that Jesus will return to earth in great glory to rescue those who believe in him.

The belief that Jesus will return isn't just the misguided opinion of certain weirdo Christians who wander round with sandwich boards preaching doom and gloom. Both the Old and the New Testaments are full of promises that Jesus will come back again to earth. Over 1,800 references appear in the Old Testament, with seventeen Old Testament books giving the exciting subject some prominence. Of the 260 chapters in the New Testament, there are more than 300 references to the Lord's return, which is one out of every thirty verses. Twenty-three of the twenty-seven New Testament books refer to this incredible event, and for every prophecy on the first coming of Jesus, there are eight on his second coming.

Jesus will return

Although there is some controversy and disagreement among Christians on how exactly it will happen, across the denominations Christians who take the Bible seriously agree that Jesus will come back in a sudden and very visible way. Jesus and others spoke about his return. Check out the words of Jesus himself in the first two examples, then the words of Paul, then John, in the third and fourth passages respectively:

> So you also must be ready, because the Son of Man will come at an hour when you do not expect him.
>
> (Matthew 24:44)

And if I go and prepare a place for you, I will come back and take you to be with me that you also may be where I am.

(John 14:3)

For the Lord himself will come down from heaven, with a loud command, with the voice of the archangel and with the trumpet call of God, and the dead in Christ will rise first.

(1 Thessalonians 4:16)

Dear friends, now we are children of God, and what we will be has not yet been made known. But we know that when he appears, we shall be like him, for we shall see him as he is.

(1 John 3:2)

It's quite clear that Jesus' return was an important hope for the early Church. It wasn't just a spiritual return, but a physical return in such a way that everyone would know, world-wide. We're not talking about a sleepy little village in the middle of nowhere equipped with a stable and manger this time. In the last book of the Bible, Revelation, John announces that Jesus will burst back into the world scene visibly and victoriously: 'Look, he is coming with the clouds and every eye will see him' (Revelation 1:7). He will come in such a dramatic way that the entire world will know that it is Jesus. Awesome, or what?! Let's look forward to Jesus' return.

We don't know when

A tourist driving through West Texas stopped at a gas station and observed a piece of rope dangling from a sign labelled 'Weather Forecaster'. 'How can you possibly tell the weather with a piece of rope?' the tourist wanted to know.

'It's simple, sonny,' came the answer in a slow, Texan drawl. 'When the rope swings back and forth, it's windy, when it gets wet, it's raining, when it's frozen stiff, it's snowing, and when it's gone – well, that's a tornado.'

Those signs indicated what the weather was going to be like. Jesus spoke about signs that would confirm his return. We don't have an exact date, but certainly many of the signs we see in our world today point to his return, sooner rather than later. Jesus told his disciples that his return was imminent. That was two thousand years ago, so if it was imminent then, just think how much more imminent it is now, in the twenty-first century.

Many groups throughout history have claimed to have known exactly when Jesus would return. The Jehovah's Witnesses claimed that Christ would return in 1874. Of course, that didn't happen, so they changed it to the belief that he came invisibly and that God's kingdom was set up on earth in 1914. Christian groups have had similar problems. They've sold houses, cars and all their possessions, resigned from work, cashed in insurance policies and taken their children out of school in preparation for his return. They've ended up with egg on their faces.

In the words of Jesus: 'No one knows about that day or hour, not even the angels in heaven, nor the Son, but only the Father. Be on guard! Be alert! You do not know when that time will come' (Mark 13:32–3). Jesus was encouraging his believers, a group which now includes us, to prepare for his return and not spend all our time on charts, calculators or computers trying to work out the precise date and time.

Signs and wonders

The Bible does mention many telltale signs that will precede Jesus' return. They include:

World-wide evangelism

'And this gospel of the kingdom will be preached in the whole world as a testimony to all nations, and then the end will come' (Matthew 24:14). According to the US Census Office, the world's population on 31 December 2000 was 6,118,958,932. Of that 6.12 billion, around 11 per cent claim to know Jesus as their personal Saviour. The rate of increase is currently around 7 per cent annually, compared to 2.6 per cent for Islam. It's estimated that between 75 and 85 per cent of people in the world have heard of Jesus, with that percentage increasing on an almost hourly basis. The entire world is getting closer to being totally evangelised.

False prophets

'At that time if anyone says to you, "Look, here is the Christ!" or, "There he is!" do not believe it. For false Christs and false prophets will appear and perform great signs and miracles to deceive even the elect – if that were possible' (Matthew 24:23–4). In our day and age, there are many who claim to be something they're not. There is a proliferation of cults and wacko religious groups who claim to be the only true religion. There are currently, in the UK alone, up to 500 active religious cults, and world-wide as many as 5,000.

I worked in a bank for five years after I left school, and very occasionally a forged note was passed over the counter by some more often than not unsuspecting customer. However good the quality of the forgery, an experienced cashier could, almost without exception, tell that the note was a fake. It wasn't because all day long they examined forged notes: it was because through the course of an average day they handled hundreds of thousands of pounds' worth of genuine notes. When you knew the real thing you could spot a fake immediately. That's one of the reasons it's so good to have good strong foundations in our faith, so we can spot wrong teaching when we hear it.

Powerful signs and phenomena in the sky

The Bible tells us that 'the sun will be darkened, and the moon will not give its light; the stars will fall from the sky, and the heavenly bodies will be shaken' (Matthew 24:29–30). You might argue that this has happened, but Jesus is speaking of something much more dramatic than eclipses, comets and meteor showers here.

Suffering and persecution

'Those will be days of distress unequalled from the beginning, when God created the world, until now – and never to be equalled again. If the Lord had not cut short those days, no one would survive. But for the sake of the elect, whom he has chosen, he has shortened them' (Mark 13:19–20). Since the birth of the Church, Christians have suffered horrendous persecution.

Some were thrown to the lions or burned at the stake. The evil Roman emperor Nero wrapped Christians in pitch and set them alight, and used them as living torches to light his gardens. He often sewed them into the skins of wild animals and set his hunting dogs upon them to tear them apart. They were tortured on the rack; molten lead was poured upon them; red hot brass plates were attached to their bodies; eyes were torn out; parts of their bodies were cut off and roasted before their very eyes; hands and feet were burned while cold water was poured over them to strengthen the agony. These things are terrible to think about, but these are the things Christians then had to be prepared for, if they took their stand for Jesus.

That was then. This is now. These days it is estimated that about 200 million Christians around the world face actual persecution, and another 350 million face discrimination and restrictions. Saudi Arabia, to give just one example, still has the unsavoury title of the world's worst persecutor of Christians. Despite the fact that there are 600,000 expatriate Christians living in the country, Saudi Arabia does not permit any practice of the Christian faith whatsoever. And that's just one example of many.

Many Jews turning to Christianity

'I do not want you to be ignorant of this mystery, brothers, so that you may not be conceited: Israel has experienced a hardening in part until the full number of the Gentiles has come in. And so all Israel will be saved' (Romans 11:25–6).

There has been much debate over exactly what this verse means. It could mean three things. First, that the majority, though not every single one, of Jews will come to know Jesus before he returns. Second, others might argue that Paul is using the term 'Israel' in the spiritual sense, i.e. Gentile (non-Jewish) and Jewish believers together will come to know Jesus. Third, it could mean that every single Jewish person without exception will be saved as they turn to accept Jesus as their Saviour.

A man of lawlessness

Concerning the coming of our Lord Jesus Christ and our being gathered to him, we ask you, brothers, not to become easily unsettled or alarmed by some prophecy, report or letter supposed to have come from us, saying that the day of the Lord has already come. Don't let anyone deceive you in any way, for that day will not come until the rebellion occurs and the man of lawlessness is revealed, the man doomed to destruction. He will oppose and will exalt himself over everything that is called God or is worshipped, so that he sets himself up in God's temple, proclaiming himself to be God.

Don't you remember that when I was with you I used to tell you these things? And now you know what is holding him back, so that he may be revealed at the proper time. For the secret power of lawlessness is already at work; but the one who now holds it back will continue to do so till he is taken out of the way. And then the lawless one will be revealed, whom the Lord Jesus will overthrow with the breath of his mouth and destroy by the splendour of his coming. The coming of the lawless one will be in accordance with the work of Satan displayed in all kinds of counterfeit miracles, signs and wonders, and in every sort of evil that deceives those who are perishing. They perish because they refused to love the truth and so be saved.

(2 Thessalonians 2:1–10)

This 'man of lawlessness' is sometimes referred to as 'the anti-christ'. I have to admit that the name 'antichrist' immediately brings to my mind thoughts of the classic 1980s horror movie trilogy *The Omen*, in which the Australian actor Sam Neill played Damian Thorne, the antichrist, with a rather fetching 666 tattoo hidden beneath his fringe. But the Bible tells us that a very real antichrist will come. Throughout history there have been many notorious figures who have been dubbed 'antichrists' because of the wickedness and destruction they have wreaked on their fellow human beings, a prime example being Hitler, who attempted to wipe out the entire Jewish race.

Antichrists like Genghis Khan, Stalin and Hitler have lived in every generation and have been hostile to everything that Jesus stands for. In the Thessalonians passage, though, Paul was talking about a completely evil man who will be Satan's tool and equipped with Satan's power. But don't panic. Paul also says that we have no need to worry if our faith in God is strong. If you've read the book of Revelation at the very end of the Bible, you'll know that God will win a great battle, the antichrist will be completely destroyed and Jesus will be victorious. Instead of being fearful and fretting, it's much more important for us to be ready and to tell others who don't yet know Jesus so that they will be prepared too.

The millennium

I'm not talking about Robbie Williams' hit single here. Because of the huge celebrations at the end of 1999, I guess there's not one person who doesn't know that the word 'millennium' means 'one thousand years'. The Bible spoke about a millennium in relationship to the return of Jesus:

> And I saw an angel coming down out of heaven, having the key to the Abyss and holding in his hand a great chain. He seized the dragon, that ancient serpent, who is the devil, or Satan, and bound him for a thousand years. He threw him into the Abyss, and locked and sealed it over him, to keep him from deceiving the nations any more until the thousand years were ended. After that, he must be set free for a short time.
>
> I saw thrones on which were seated those who had been given authority to judge. And I saw the souls of those who had been beheaded because of their testimony for Jesus and because of the word of God. They had not worshipped the beast or his image and had not received his mark on their foreheads or their hands. They came to life and reigned with Christ for a thousand years.
>
> (Revelation 20:1–5)

John's writings in Revelation were written in the 'apocalyptic' form, a style of Jewish writing that uses incredible symbolic imagery to communicate hope that God will triumph to those suffering persecution. It was around AD 95 and John was writing in exile on an island called Patmos, which was just off the coast of what's now Turkey. He was writing for Christians everywhere, but specifically to seven churches in Asia who were suffering incredible persecution. As for what this passage means, I have to admit that Christians can't really agree. Over hundreds of years, top Bible scholars have disagreed over what the 'millennium' actually means. I can't do justice to this tricky subject in a matter of a few hundred words – indeed, I have real problems merely getting my tongue around the pronunciation of the words – but let me have a go and attempt to explain the main schools of thought to you. Here goes.

Postmillennialism

'Post' means 'after', so you don't need a GCSE in English to figure out that this term means 'after the millennium'. The view means that the effectiveness and growth of the Church will increase in phenomenal ways so that more of the world will be Christians. At the end of this thousand-year period, Satan will be unleashed on the earth one last time, until Jesus comes back and defeats him.

Premillennialism

This position holds that Jesus will come back before the millennium and his return will start the millennium period. His return will happen after the Church experiences a time of great suffering and tribulation. Jesus will come back to earth to establish his kingdom on earth, and Christians, including those who have died, will reign with Jesus for a thousand years. Many unbelievers will become Christians during this period and there will be peace on earth. During this time Satan will be thrown into the bottomless pit (see Revelation 20:1–3) so that he will have no influence on people during the millennium period.

Pretribulational premillennialism

I hope this isn't getting too complicated. I mention this spin-off of premillennialism because this view has become popular in the last couple of centuries, particularly in America and the UK, and is often referred to as the 'Rapture'. I've even seen car stickers that state, 'In the event of the Rapture this car will be without a driver.' So if you happen to see a driverless car parked somewhere with that sticker in the back window, then either the Rapture has happened and you've unfortunately been left behind, or the owner has nipped into a shop.

All joking apart, this view means that Jesus will return before the millennium (premillennialism), but also before the tribulation (pretribulational) and then will secretly and suddenly take all the Christians out of the world:

> For the Lord himself will come down from heaven, with a loud command, with the voice of the archangel and with the trumpet call of God, and the dead in Christ will rise first. After that, we who are still alive and are left will be caught up together with them in the clouds to meet the Lord in the air. And so we will be with the Lord for ever.
>
> (1 Thessalonians 4:16–17)

Jesus then returns to heaven with all the Christians, and they miss a seven-year period of tribulation. It'll be during this short period of suffering and pain that many will come to trust in Jesus for the first time. Many of the signs I've already discussed will happen, and these will culminate in Jesus' return at the end of the tribulation with all the believers to reign on earth for a thousand years. After this millennium period, Satan will be defeated for the final time.

Amillennialism

If you're still with me, let's look at probably the simplest view, so feel free to breathe a huge sigh of relief! Those who hold to this view reckon that we're actually living in the millennium period here and now. They would claim that the millennium period is symbolic of Jesus' ascension into heaven and his second coming, and that the thousand-year period is simply a figure of speech. This period of time, however, will end with Jesus' second coming, when there will be a resurrection of both believers and unbelievers. Christians will go to heaven and unbelievers will face judgment.

Glorification

As part and parcel of the second coming, Christians also believe that Jesus will raise the bodies of all believers who have died throughout the ages and he will reunite them with their souls. At the same time he will give all Christians who are still alive new perfect bodies, like his own. This process of receiving brand new, resurrected bodies is known as 'glorification'.

The main New Testament passage on glorification comes in Paul's lengthy letter to the Christians in Corinth. The entire account is taken from 1 Corinthians 15:12–58, where Paul explains that our new bodies will be without pain, sickness and disability: 'Listen, I tell you a mystery: We will not all sleep, but we will all be changed – in a flash, in the twinkling of an eye, at the last trumpet. For the trumpet will sound, the dead will be raised imperishable, and we will be changed' (1 Corinthians 15:51–2).

Prior to this, Paul also explored this line of teaching in an earlier letter to the church in Thessalonica:

> Brothers, we do not want you to be ignorant about those who fall asleep, or to grieve like the rest of men, who have no hope. We believe that Jesus died and rose again and so we believe that God will bring with Jesus those who have fallen asleep in him. According to the Lord's own word, we tell you that we who are still alive, who are left till the coming of the Lord, will certainly not precede those who have fallen asleep. For the Lord himself will come down from heaven, with a loud command, with the voice of the archangel and with the trumpet call of God, and the dead in Christ will rise first. After that, we who are still alive and are left will be caught up together with them in the clouds to meet the Lord in the air. And so we will be with the Lord for ever.
>
> (1 Thessalonians 4:13–17)

So there we have, in a nutshell, the main views about the second coming of Jesus and the millennium. I'm sure that many biblical scholars and professors of theology will be shaking their heads, and tut-tutting at my simplistic and feeble attempts to explain major issues in a few paragraphs. Whatever your view on the sequence of events might be, all Bible-believing Christians will be united in believing the key points, and that's what really matters:

1 Jesus will return.
2 Jesus will defeat Satan.
3 Jesus will reign for ever.

Whatever your specific view – and you might not even have one – be ready and in anticipation that Jesus is coming back. When times are hard, remember that eventually all evil will be gone: 'He will wipe every tear from their eyes. There will be no more death or mourning or crying or pain, for the old order of things has passed away' (Revelation 21:4).

One day, maybe even quite soon, paradise lost will be paradise regained, and Jesus will be victorious.

Delving deeper

How will Jesus return?
1 Matthew 24:44
2 John 14:3
3 Acts 1:11
4 1 Thessalonians 4:16
5 Hebrews 9:28
6 2 Peter 3:10
7 Revelation 1:7

When will Jesus return?
1 Matthew 24:44
2 Matthew 25:13
3 Mark 13:32–3
4 Luke 12:40
5 James 5:8

What will our glorified (resurrected) bodies be like?

1 Matthew 13:43
2 Romans 8:29
3 1 Corinthians 15:43
4 1 Corinthians 15:49
5 1 John 3:2

Could Jesus return very soon?

1 Matthew 24:36–9
2 Matthew 25:13
3 Mark 13:32–3
4 Luke 12:40
5 1 Corinthians 16:22

Memory verses

According to the Lord's own word, we tell you that we who are still alive, who are left till the coming of the Lord, will certainly not precede those who have fallen asleep. For the Lord himself will come down from heaven, with a loud command, with the voice of the archangel and with the trumpet call of God, and the dead in Christ will rise first. After that, we who are still alive and are left will be caught up together with them in the clouds to meet the Lord in the air. And so we will be with the Lord for ever. Therefore encourage each other with these words.

(1 Thessalonians 4:15–18)

16

Final Judgment

Nobody can judge men but God, and we can hardly obtain a higher or more reverent view of God than that which represents him to us as judging men with perfect knowledge, unperplexed certainty, and undisturbed compassion.

Frederick William Faber

I was summoned to attend court many years ago, and have to admit that the whole process was rather nerve-racking. I was so nervous and my hands were so clammy that I dropped my copious notes all over the floor, and it was quite a sight to witness the poor clerk of the court scrabbling on the floor attempting to retrieve them and reassemble them in the correct order. At the end of the proceedings the judge decided the level of punishment and sentence that was appropriate.

Judgment Day

Eternal judgment is when Jesus decides the ultimate destiny of all people on earth. The Bible tells us this judgment will take place after the millennium and the final rebellion against God that goes with it:

> Then I saw a great white throne and him who was seated on it. Earth and sky fled from his presence, and there was no place for them. And I saw the dead, great and small, standing before the throne, and books were opened. Another book was opened, which is the book of life. The dead were judged according to what they had done as recorded in the books. The sea gave up the dead that were in it, and death and Hades gave up the dead that were in them, and each person was judged according to what he had done. Then death and Hades were thrown into the lake of fire. The lake of fire is the second death. If anyone's name was not found written in the book of life, he was thrown into the lake of fire.
>
> (Revelation 20:11–15)

But it's not just John who wrote about eternal judgment. Here are just four other examples for you to get your teeth into:

> But I tell you that men will have to give account on the day of judgment for every careless word they have spoken. For by your words you will be acquitted, and by your words you will be condemned.
>
> (Matthew 12:36–7)

> Therefore judge nothing before the appointed time; wait till the Lord comes. He will bring to light what is hidden in darkness and will expose the motives of men's hearts. At that time each will receive his praise from God.
>
> (1 Corinthians 4:5)

> See, the Lord is coming with thousands upon thousands of his holy ones to judge everyone, and to convict all the

ungodly of all the ungodly acts they have done in the ungodly way, and of all the harsh words ungodly sinners have spoken against him.

(Jude 14–15)

In Matthew 25:31–46 Jesus talks about eternal judgment through a story in which he uses sheep and goats to describe believers and unbelievers. Both sets of animals would often have spent days together grazing in the same fields, but, of course, when it was the time to shear the sheep they would have been separated. Also, through the story Jesus encourages us to treat others as if they were Jesus. He encourages us to feed the hungry, give the thirsty something to drink, give the homeless somewhere to stay, clothe those who have nothing to wear, nurse the sick and visit those in prison. In other words, what we do for others demonstrates what we believe.

How judgment is decided

To decide judgment, you need a judge. It is clear from what the Bible says that everyone will be judged. We can read that Jesus will be that judge:

For as the Father has life in himself, so he has granted the Son to have life in himself. And he has given him authority to judge because he is the Son of Man.

(John 5:26–7)

He commanded us to preach to the people and to testify that he is the one whom God appointed as judge of the living and the dead.

(Acts 10:42)

In the presence of God and of Christ Jesus, who will judge the living and the dead.

(2 Timothy 4:1)

Believers will be judged

Paul explained to the Christians in Rome how each person is accountable to Jesus for their own sins. He urged them to stop criticising and judging other Christians. Jesus will deal with them himself:

> You, then, why do you judge your brother? Or why do you look down on your brother? For we will all stand before God's judgment seat. It is written:
>
> > 'As surely as I live,' says the Lord,
> > 'Every knee will bow before me;
> > every tongue will confess to God.'
>
> So then, each of us will give an account of himself to God.
> (Romans 14:10–12)

We know that Jesus will judge us all, but if we have truly repented and are real followers of his then we needn't worry unduly – after all, our sins have been forgiven. This should give every Christian an unequivocal mandate to live for Jesus in a way that pleases him. That should be our goal, so through our lives and actions let's, in the words of Jesus, 'Store up for yourselves treasures in heaven, where moth and rust do not destroy, and where thieves do not break in and steal' (Matthew 6:20).

Unbelievers will be judged

Those who don't believe in Jesus will be judged by him on what they have done in their lives. It seems to me that it's true that you reap what you sow, and this is what Paul describes for those who don't follow Jesus and his teachings: 'But because of your stubbornness and your unrepentant heart, you are storing up wrath against yourself for the day of God's wrath, when his righteous judgment will be revealed. God "will give to each person according to what he has done" ' (Romans 2:5–7). On Judgment Day every single unbeliever will be judged on their lives. Every last wrong word, thought and action will be remembered and taken into account. It will all be in the open.

Please don't think it's not fair that God will be so harsh on those who don't love Jesus. God has to be fair. He made the rules at the beginning of time in Eden, and ever since then humankind has tried to bend and break those rules. God's not unfair. As we've seen throughout this book, he sent the most precious thing he had, his one and only Son, into the world to give people a lifeline through which they could be saved.

But God is never going to force anyone to love him or follow him. It was the great preacher A.W. Tozer who summed up God's perfect justice with these words: 'God's compassion flows out of his goodness, and goodness without justice is not goodness. God spares us because he is good, but he could not be good if he were not just.' If people have deliberately chosen to live without God in this life and to go their own selfish, sinful way, then they will have to face eternity without him too.

Angels will be judged

I have to admit I didn't realise this until I started writing this book. So maybe my foundations weren't as deep and strong as I thought they were. Angels are spiritual beings that God created at the beginning of time, so you can forget the image of winged people in white nightdresses with a fluorescent ring doughnut hovering over their heads. We read at the start of this book how Satan and a number of angels rebelled against God. The Apostle Peter taught that God 'did not spare angels when they sinned, but sent them to hell, putting them into gloomy dungeons to be held for judgment' (2 Peter 2:4).

Theologians aren't altogether sure whether righteous angels will be judged as well. I guess it's one of those things we'll know when we get to heaven. In the meantime, what is clear is that everyone – both physical beings like us human beings and spiritual beings like angels – will have to give an account of themselves and their actions one day at the end of time before God. The fact that everyone will be judged, and those who don't believe will be punished, should give us another reason for evangelism. God wants no one to die without knowing him: 'not wanting anyone to perish, but everyone to come to repentance' (2 Peter 3:9). This should give us a great urgency in sharing our faith with as many as we can.

Hell

To really cheer you up, I'm going to finish this chapter by looking at hell. Hell is tied in with eternal judgment, so it's important and appropriate to attempt to explain what it is and what it's not. Don't worry, the good news about heaven deserves its own chapter and follows immediately after this one.

Powerful imagery comes to mind when hell is mentioned. Pictures of miserable sinners being barbecued in lakes of burning sulphur, with Satan prodding people with a sharp pitchfork while dressed in a one-piece red leotard and floor-length cape, easily come to mind. I prefer the altogether more realistic image that the English author C.S. Lewis painted: 'We must picture hell as a state where everyone is perpetually concerned about his own dignity and advancement, where everyone has a grievance, and where everyone lives the deadly serious passions of envy, self-importance, and resentment.' Jesus referred to a place called hell in a number of ways:

He will reply, 'I tell you the truth, whatever you did not do for one of the least of these, you did not do for me.'

> Then they will go away to eternal punishment, but the righteous to eternal life.
>
> (Matthew 25:45–6)

> If your hand causes you to sin, cut it off. It is better for you to enter life maimed than with two hands to go into hell, where the fire never goes out.
>
> (Mark 9:43)

The book of Revelation reaffirms the idea that hell is an actual place:

> A third angel followed them and said in a loud voice: 'If anyone worships the beast and his image and receives his mark on the forehead or on the hand, he, too, will drink of the wine of God's fury, which has been poured full strength into the cup of his wrath. He will be tormented with burning sulphur in the presence of the holy angels and of the Lamb. And the smoke of their torment rises for ever and ever. There is no rest day or night for those who worship the beast and his image, or for anyone who receives the mark of his name.
>
> (Revelation 14:9–11)

This is serious stuff, and these verses are probably the most frightening in the book of Revelation. It shows how terrible it will be for those who reject God's offer of eternal life through Jesus.

Annihilationism

There is another viewpoint that I'll mention here, albeit very briefly. Certain theologians would disagree that those who go to hell will suffer punishment for eternity. It could be argued that a number of verses suggest the wicked will be destroyed: for example, 'While people are saying, "Peace and safety," destruction will come on them suddenly, as labour pains on a pregnant woman, and they will not escape' (1 Thessalonians 5:3). They would concur that those who have rejected Jesus' teaching will go to hell, but only for a time, after which God will totally annihilate them so they no longer exist. This teaching, not surprisingly, is known as 'annihilationism'.

Purgatory

It would also be appropriate to talk about purgatory briefly. Apparently, purgatory is a place where the souls of Christians go to have their sins further purified before they go to heaven. We have to be very clear in saying that this doctrine, which is used by the Catholic Church, is not taught anywhere in the Bible whatsoever. If purgatory is to be believed, then what Jesus achieved through his death and resurrection to wash us clean from all our sin wasn't enough. Christians believe that once they die, although their physical body is left on earth, their soul – or spirit – immediately goes to be with God in heaven.

On 4th July 1854, a notorious English criminal, Charlie Peace, was hanged in London. As the condemned man was marched to the gallows, an Anglican priest walked behind him and read the following words from his prayer book: 'Those who die without Christ experience hell, which is the pain of forever dying without the release which death itself can bring.'

As those chilling words were read, Charlie Peace stopped in his tracks, turned to the priest and shouted in his face, 'Do you really believe that? Do you?!'

The priest, taken aback for one moment, stammered for a few seconds and then said, 'Well . . . I . . . I suppose I do.'

'Well I don't,' said Peace, 'but if I did, I would get down on my hands and knees and crawl all over Great Britain, even if it were paved with broken glass, if I could rescue just one person from what you have just told me.'

God never plans to send anyone to hell. Hell wasn't created for people, it was created for the devil and his evil angels. People go there by their own free choice. The very existence of hell should give every single Christian the greatest possible incentive to explain the good news of the gospel to as many as we can. Let's do it.

Delving deeper

How will judgment happen?
1　John 12:48
2　Romans 1:18
3　2 Timothy 4:1
4　Hebrews 9:27
5　Jude 14–15

Will everyone be judged?
1　Romans 2:6
2　Romans 14:10
3　Romans 14:12
4　2 Corinthians 5:10
5　1 Peter 1:17

How will judgment be decided?
1　Matthew 10:32–3
2　John 3:16–21
3　John 5:24
4　Romans 2:8
5　Romans 6:23

Memory verses

So we make it our goal to please him, whether we are at home in the body or away from it. For we must all appear before the judgment seat of Christ, that each one may receive what is due him for the things done while in the body, whether good or bad.

(2 Corinthians 5:9–10)

17

Heaven

Heaven is the perfectly ordered and harmonious enjoyment of God and of one another in God.

St Augustine of Hippo

Once there was an old man who every day would take long walks with the Lord. On these walks, he and the Lord God would talk about all kinds of things – about the important times in the old man's life: when he met his wife, the birth of his children, birthdays and other special events. One day while they were out walking for an especially long time, the Lord looked at the old man and said, 'We are closer to my house than we are to yours. Why don't you just come home with me?' And that is what he did.

On 16th June 2002, *The Mail on Sunday*'s one-word headline was 'Heaven', though on closer inspection I discovered that it wasn't a story about spiritual matters but the report of the England football team's trouncing of Denmark, 3–0, in the 2002 World Cup. John Lennon wrote a song about heaven, called 'Imagine'. It was a beautiful song about peace all over the world, with no fighting, no racism and other wonderful ideals, but the title summed his song up – because without Jesus all you could do was imagine.

There's no doubt about it, 'heaven' certainly does conjure up some interesting ideas and images. The image I've often had is of thousands of old people, wearing white negligees, fluttering their wings while sitting on fluffy clouds playing gold harps and singing 'Kum ba Yah'. Over at the entrance a burly bouncer, called St Peter, sits with a clipboard at the pearly gates of heaven checking names on his list to see whether people are allowed in or not.

I don't know how different that is to your view of heaven. Incidentally, the St Peter idea comes from the words of Jesus, 'I will give you the keys of the kingdom of heaven' (Matthew 16:19). Now he didn't physically give him a set of front-door keys and appoint him as a heavenly receptionist or doorman. These 'keys' were given to him symbolically as a sign of his spiritual authority. After Jesus returned to heaven, Peter became a tremendous preacher and saw many miracles happen through his work. You could say he opened the doors of heaven to thousands of Jews on the day of Pentecost, then some years later to non-Jews, Gentiles. He was also miraculously released from prison with others, before he was executed for his faith in Jesus.

But I digress. The biblical view of heaven has much more to it than just living with God for ever. That is, of course, a wonderful aspect of what heaven is, but in the words of funny-man Jimmy Cricket . . . there's more! God promised a new heaven and a new earth, but more of that later in this chapter.

What is heaven?

Let's begin by looking at heaven as we know it now, though I have to admit we don't really know that much. Indeed, heaven is a bit of a mystery to us. His Holiness Pope John Paul II rejected the idea of heaven as a place, calling it instead, a 'state of being'. In July 1999, he told pilgrims in St Peter's Square, Rome, that it was 'close communion and full intimacy with God'. The Pontiff added: 'The heaven in which we will find ourselves is neither an abstraction nor a physical place among clouds. It is a blessed community of those who remained faithful to Jesus Christ and are now at one with his glory.'

I have to say I find that a bit confusing. I personally believe the Bible teaches that heaven is an 'actual' place. In Isaiah 66:1 we read: 'This is what the LORD says: "Heaven is my throne," ' and Jesus said when he taught us to pray the Lord's Prayer, 'Our Father in heaven, hallowed be your name' (Matthew 6:9). Later in the New Testament we read that Jesus has now 'gone into heaven and is at God's right hand – with angels, authorities and powers in submission to him' (1 Peter 3:22). Quite simply, heaven is the place where God lives.

As has been already mentioned, Christians believe that when they die, although their physical body remains on earth and is either buried or cremated, their soul goes straight away into the presence of God. Jesus said to the thief who was crucified on the cross next to him: 'I tell you the truth, today you will be with me in paradise' (Luke 23:43). It happens immediately.

Heaven is real

It was the former slave-trader and great hymn-writer John Newton who wrote: 'If I ever reach heaven, I expect to find three wonders there: first, to meet some I had not thought to see there; second, to miss some I had expected to see there; and third, the greatest wonder of all, to find myself there.' What a great quote. He's right, heaven is going to be a wonderful place, and that's what the New Testament teaches, that heaven is an actual place.

Jesus promised his followers, which includes you and me: 'In my Father's house are many rooms; if it were not so, I would have told you. I am going there to prepare a place for you. And if I go and prepare a place for you, I will come back and take you to be with me that you also may be where I am' (John 14:2–3). He was going to that place to be with his Father, but one day will come back again to take us with him to that very same place. More of that later.

After he had died and rose again, Jesus some forty days later ascended into a place called heaven: 'While he was blessing them, he left them and was taken up into heaven. Then they worshipped him and returned to Jerusalem with great joy. And they stayed continually at the temple, praising God' (Luke 24:51–3).

When this happened the angels explained to the dumbstruck disciples what was happening and where Jesus was going: ' "Men of Galilee," they said, "why do you stand here looking into the sky? This same Jesus, who has been taken from you into heaven, will come back in the same way you have seen him go into heaven" ' (Acts 1:11). Jesus was certainly going to a place, not some ethereal state of mind.

As the early Church grew it faced much persecution. Stephen, just before he was stoned to death, 'full of the Holy Spirit, looked up to heaven and saw the glory of God, and Jesus standing at the right hand of God. "Look," he said, "I see heaven open and the Son of Man standing at the right hand of God" ' (Acts 7:55–6).

Those are just a few examples that lead me to believe that heaven is most definitely a place – though, of course, where it is precisely is a mystery. Historically we've believed that it was up in the sky somewhere, because the Bible always talks about people ascending up into heaven or coming down from heaven – like the angels in Jacob's dream: 'He had a dream in which he saw a stairway resting on the earth, with its top reaching to heaven, and the angels of God were ascending and descending on it' (Genesis 28:12).

Heaven could be on one of the stars. I don't know, none of us knows. The Bible certainly doesn't give an address or a map reference. Maybe it is a star in a far-off galaxy. I do know, because I've been told, that on a clear night you can see over two thousand stars in the heavens. With a good pair of binoculars about a hundred times as many will be visible. With even better and more powerful equipment you can see even more. We know about 30,000 million suns in our galaxy, and then there are the ones we don't know about in our and other galaxies. Perhaps heaven is on one of these stars. Personally, it really doesn't worry me one little bit. Christians know that heaven is where Jesus is going to be, and that it's going to be wonderful because he's there – and that's good enough for me.

Getting to heaven

The American evangelist Billy Graham said this about heaven:

> I'm not going to heaven because I've preached to great crowds of people. I'm going to heaven because Christ died on that cross. None of us are going to heaven because we're good. And we're not going to heaven because we've worked. We're not going to heaven because we pray and accept Christ. We're going to heaven because of what he did on the cross. All I have to do is receive him. And it's so easy to receive Christ that millions stumble over its sheer simplicity.

It really is as easy as that.

That's why the New Testament encourages believers to face death not with foreboding and fear, but with excitement that we are going home to be with Jesus. Christians don't need to be scared of death. The Bible couldn't make it clearer: 'For I am convinced that neither death nor life, neither angels nor demons, neither the present nor the future, nor any powers, neither height nor depth, nor anything else in all creation, will be able to separate us from the love of God that is in Christ Jesus our Lord' (Romans 8:38–9).

Heaven is just for those who love Jesus and follow him. Unbelievers don't go to heaven. The great Apostle Paul was heartbroken just thinking about some of his friends and colleagues who had chosen to reject Jesus and his teachings: 'I speak the truth in Christ – I am not lying, my conscience confirms it in the Holy Spirit – I have great sorrow and unceasing anguish in my heart. For I could wish that I myself were cursed and cut off from Christ for the sake of my brothers, those of my own race' (Romans 9:1–3).

Of course, no funeral is going to be a bundle of laughs, but at Christian funerals, amid the tears, sorrow and sense of loss, there is a hope and joy that the person has gone to be with Jesus. Paul knew that death was not the end. This is what he wrote from his prison cell as he himself faced imminent execution: 'For to me, to live is Christ and to die is gain. If I am to go on living in the body, this will mean fruitful labour for me. Yet what shall I choose? I do not know! I am torn between the two: I desire to depart and be with Christ, which is better by far' (Philippians 1:21–3).

It would be unreal not to cry or mourn for a loved one. Jesus 'wept' (John 11:35) when one of his closest friends, Lazarus, died. But our sadness should be mixed with grateful thanks to God for that person's life, and that they loved Jesus and have gone to spend eternity with him. Heaven is a place prepared for those who are prepared for it.

New heaven and new earth

Christians believe that when they die they immediately go into the presence of God in heaven, as I've already described, but earlier I alluded to something even greater than that. If you think the heaven we know in our current times sounds wonderful, then get a load of the words of John, who described a new heaven and earth where Christians would live with God after the final judgment:

> Then I saw a new heaven and a new earth, for the first heaven and the first earth had passed away, and there was no longer any sea. I saw the Holy City, the new Jerusalem,

coming down out of heaven from God, prepared as a bride beautifully dressed for her husband. And I heard a loud voice from the throne saying, 'Now the dwelling of God is with men, and he will live with them. They will be his people, and God himself will be with them and be their God.'

(Revelation 21:1–3)

This place John describes sounds awesome. It is beautiful. God is there. Look what else Revelation 21 and 22 reveals:

1 There will be no more death, mourning, crying or pain (21:4)
2 Everything will be new (21:5)
3 There will be a fountain of the water of life (21:6)
4 The city will shine like the glory of God. Its brilliance will be like precious jewels (21:11)
5 It will be so vast it can hold every believer (21:15–17)
6 It will be constructed of precious jewels that will last for ever (21:18–21)
7 Nothing or no one evil or impure will be there (21:27)
8 There will be trees and crops that can be eaten (22:2–3)
9 We'll be in the presence of God for all eternity (22:3)

It sounds amazing. However hard things are now, in the future a new heaven and earth is waiting. It should give us a real hope and a future for the world. It's good news – and never forget, good news is for sharing.

In the book of Revelation, God is described as the Alpha and Omega – the beginning and the end. Human history began in Genesis and it ends in Revelation. It started and finishes in paradise. In the beginning in Eden, Adam and Eve talked to God, were tempted by a snake, and evil came into the world. At the end, in Revelation, people worship God face to face in a perfect city without sin. When God sent Adam and Eve out of

Eden he set mighty angels – called cherubim – to guard the gates of Eden (Genesis 3:24). Now at the end of time the angels stand at the gates to open them in welcome. God has been involved throughout the whole process and now paradise has been recreated. It's going to be fantastic.

Delving deeper

Is heaven a place?
1 Genesis 28:12
2 John 14:2
3 John 14:3
4 Acts 1:11
5 Acts 7:55–6

How will the earth be changed and renewed?
1 Romans 8:19–21
2 Hebrews 1:11–12
3 Hebrews 12:26–7
4 2 Peter 3:10
5 Revelation 20:11

What will the new heaven and earth be like?
1 Matthew 6:19–21
2 Luke 22:18
3 Colossians 1:10
4 2 Peter 3:11–13
5 Revelation 19:9
6 Revelation 21:27
7 Revelation 22:5

Memory verses

> I eagerly expect and hope that I will in no way be ashamed, but will have sufficient courage so that now as always Christ

will be exalted in my body, whether by life or by death. For to me, to live is Christ and to die is gain. If I am to go on living in the body, this will mean fruitful labour for me. Yet what shall I choose? I do not know! I am torn between the two: I desire to depart and be with Christ, which is better by far; but it is more necessary for you that I remain in the body.

(Philippians 1:20–4)

18

And Finally . . .

> I've read the last page of the Bible. It's all going to turn out
> all right.
>
> *Billy Graham*

I recently read a story about a woman who died and went to
heaven where she met St Peter at the famous pearly gates. Upon
her being taken into heaven, Peter began to show her around.
One immediate thing the lady couldn't help noticing was that
on the walls of an enormous warehouse were thousands of
clocks. All of these clocks were ticking away but at different
rates. On closer inspection the woman then noticed that under
each clock was a name plate with a name engraved on it.
Curiosity soon got the better of her and she asked the significance of all this. Peter informed her that each clock was designed
to keep track of an individual still on earth. Each time the person
represented by the clock committed a sin, the hands on the
clock made a complete revolution.

Upon closer examination the lady began to recognise the
names of some of her friends and acquaintances. After searching
for her husband's name and not finding it, she enquired as to
where she might find his clock. St Peter replied, 'Oh, his clock.

Well, we moved his into the office and we're using it as a fan.'

Of course, the story isn't true, but I like it anyway so it's stayed in. When we become Christians, life doesn't suddenly become easy. We don't all wander through the rest of our lives with a permanent dopey grin on our faces. Bible study isn't always a great joy, and you might be like me and occasionally fall asleep while praying. I've been a Christian since a Boys' Brigade camp in 1980 and I love God dearly, but have to admit I'm not always a great Christian. If I'm really honest, I'm still a right misery sometimes. I lose my temper, get irritated and wound up all too easily, snap at my wife and shout at my children. I sometimes wake up and even doubt the existence of God.

I'm sure I'm not alone. Most of us doubt from time to time – and let's face it, we all mess up. It's so easy through a careless word or action to hurt others. We all get things wrong and failure is never pleasant. But Jesus never promised anyone an easy road. It certainly isn't enjoyable to lose a job, see a relationship go pear-shaped or fail exams.

Jesus didn't smile from ear to ear and crack jokes as he was butchered to death at Calvary. But he knew it was part of God's perfect will and plan. We all struggle in our Christian lives at one point or another – it's not one long spiritual high. There are boring bits and hard times, too. But whatever happens in our lives we need to know and believe that ultimately God is in control. The future's bright. The future is exciting. Many people live in dread of the future, but why should we? The unknown puts adventure into life. The unexpected around the corner gives a sense of anticipation and surprise. God has an exciting plan and purpose for your life and he wants to use you, however ordinary or insignificant you might feel.

Jesus' first disciples certainly weren't a bunch of spiritual superstars. Instead they were a motley crew of very ordinary men from varied backgrounds, with different occupations and personalities. James, John, Simon and Andrew were fishermen. They probably owned their own boats and had flourishing businesses, yet they left it all to follow Jesus. Matthew was a very wealthy tax collector, and Simon the Zealot belonged to a nationalist group whose aim was to overthrow the Romans and free Israel. Judas Iscariot, the traitor, was the group's dodgy treasurer, and Philip was the neighbour of Andrew and the loudmouth, Peter. Andrew in turn told Bartholomew that he had found the Messiah. Thomas was nicknamed 'Doubting Thomas', but he stopped doubting after he had met the risen Jesus. Indeed, legend tells us that Thomas was killed by a lance at Coromandel in the East Indies, rather than refute his faith. We don't know much about James and the other Judas, apart from the fact that they and the others were ordinary people that Jesus chose to alter the course of human history.

However you might view yourself, God sees tremendous potential in you and has a wonderful plan for your life. You can make a difference. It's not ability that God looks for, it's avail-ability. The Christian life is like an exciting journey and you'll soon find that once you're moving in co-operation with God and going in the right direction, things will fall into place: ' "For I know the plans I have for you," declares the LORD, "plans to prosper you and not to harm you, plans to give you hope and a future" ' (Jeremiah 29:11).

Don't feel that you need to wear black, look miserable and grow a beard. Being serious, wearing sandals in December or owning the largest tambourine money can buy certainly isn't a sign of being spiritual. Don't let religious people squeeze you into a straitjacket of rules and regulations. Jesus came to give us life, and life in all its wonderful abundance, so enjoy it. Have a laugh on a Sunday. Be spontaneous. Admit your doubts and uncertainties. Have fun. Be normal, enjoy life and always keep your focus on Jesus.

We may not know what the future holds, but we know who holds the future. Jesus is coming back soon. 'Soon' could mean any moment. Let's be ready.

Therefore let us leave the elementary teachings about Christ and go on to maturity, not laying again the foundation of repentance from acts that lead to death, and of faith in God, instruction about baptisms, the laying on of hands, the resurrection of the dead, and eternal judgment. And God permitting, we will do so.

(Hebrews 6:1–3)

Appendix 1
The Parables of Jesus

Parable	Matthew	Mark	Luke
A lamp under a bowl	5:14–15	4:21–2	8:16
Houses on rock and sand	7:24–7		6:47–9
New cloth on an old coat	9:16	2:21	5:36
New wine in old wineskins	9:17	2:22	5:37–8
The sower and different soils	13:3–8	4:3–8	8:5–8
Mustard seed	13:31–2	4:30–2	13:18–19
Weeds	13:24–30		
Yeast	13:33		13:20–1
Hidden treasure	13:44		
A pearl	13:45–6		
A net	13:47–8		
Lost sheep	18:12–13		15:4–6
An unforgiving servant	18:23–34		
Workers in the vineyard	20:1–16		
Two sons	21:28–31		
Wicked tenants	21:33–41	12:1–9	20:9–16
A wedding feast	22:2–14		
A fig tree	24:32–3	13:28–9	21:29–32
Ten bridesmaids	25:1–13		
Silver coins	25:14–30		

Parable	Matthew	Mark	Luke
Gold coins			19:12–27
Sheep and goats	25:31–6		
The growing seed		4:26–9	
A moneylender			7:41–3
The Good Samaritan			10:30–7
A friend in need			11:5–8
The rich fool			12:16–21
Watchful servants			12:35–40
The faithful servant			12:42–8
The unfruitful fig tree			13:6–9
The best places at a wedding feast			14:7–14
A great feast and reluctant guests			14:16–24
Counting the cost			14:28–33
A lost coin			15:8–10
The lost son			15:11–32
The shrewd manager			16:1–8
The rich man and Lazarus			16:19–31
The master and his servant			17:7–10
The widow and the judge			18:2–5
The Pharisee and the tax collector			18:10–14

Appendix 2
The Miracles of Jesus

	Matthew	Mark	Luke	John
Healing				
A man with a skin disease	8:2–3	1:40–2	5:12–13	
The Roman officer's servant	8:5–13		7:1–10	
Peter's mother-in-law	8:14–15	1:30–1	4:38–9	
The paralysed man	9:2–7	2:3–12	5:18–25	
A sick woman	9:20–2	5:25–9	8:43–8	
Two blind men following Jesus	9:27–31			
The man with a paralysed hand	12:10–13	3:1–5	6:6–10	
The Canaanite woman's daughter	15:21–8	7:24–30		
The boy with epilepsy	17:14–18	9:17–29	9:38–43	
Two blind men at the roadside	20:29–34			
Blind Bartimaeus		10:46–52	18:35–43	
The deaf mute		7:31–7		
A blind man at Bethsaida		8:22–6		
A crippled woman			13:11–13	

	Matthew	Mark	Luke	John
A man with swollen limbs			14:1–4	
Ten men with a skin disease			17:11–19	
The High Priest's slave			22:50–1	
The official's son at Capernaum				4:46–54
A sick man at the pool of Bethesda				5:1–9

Freed from demon possession

	Matthew	Mark	Luke	John
Two men from Gadarenes	8:28–34	5:1–15	8:27–35	
A dumb man	9:32–3			
A blind and dumb man	12:22		11:14	
A man in the synagogue		1:23–6	4:33–5	

Command over nature

	Matthew	Mark	Luke	John
The calming of the storm	8:23–7	4:37–41	8:22–5	
Walking on the water	14:25	6:48–51		6:19–21
Five thousand people fed	14:15–21	6:35–44	9:12–17	6:5–13
Four thousand people fed	15:32–8	8:1–9		
The coin in a fish's mouth	17:24–7			
The withered fig tree	21:18–22	11:12–25		
The catch of fish			5:1–11	
Water turned into wine				2:1–11
Another catch of fish				21:1–11

Raising the dead

	Matthew	Mark	Luke	John
Jairus' daughter	9:18–25	5:22–42	8:41–56	
The widow's son at Nain			7:11–15	
Lazarus				11:1–44

Glossary

The letter that follows was sent home with some American high school students. This is what it said: 'Our school's cross-graded, multi-ethnic, individualized learning program is designed to enhance the concept of an open-ended learning program on the continuum of academically enriched learning, using the identified intellectually gifted child as the agent of his own learning.'

One rather perplexed parent sent back a note which read, 'I have a college degree, speak two foreign languages and four Indian dialects – but I haven't the faintest idea what you are talking about.'

As you reach the final few pages of this book, I hope you've understood most of what I've been talking about. I've done my very best to make some complicated theories and beliefs as easy to understand as I possibly can. To help further, particularly for the reader who skips back and forth throughout the book, I thought I'd take this opportunity to put together a short glossary of many of the more important words I've used in this book.

You'll also notice I've added other less significant words as well. I thought it might be fun and maybe even helpful to interpret some of the strange phrases and colloquialisms that many Christians use today. I guess it's easy for any group of people of like mind to use jargon – well, I've tried to explain some of these often daft terms as well. They're the words or phrases in italics. Hope it helps.

Amillennialism
The teaching that the bodily reign of Jesus on earth, prior to the final judgment, won't be a literal thousand-year time period. This view suggests that we are currently living in the millennium.

Angel
Forget the white dress, tiny fluttering wings and a glowing halo. Angels are spiritual beings that have been created by God.

Annihilationism
The belief that after they die, unbelievers experience the anger of God for a period and then they are completely destroyed or 'annihilated'.

Antichrist
Described by John as 'the man of lawlessness', this man is evil personified and will appear on earth before Jesus returns to earth for the final time. The antichrist will cause much pain, suffering and persecution before being totally and utterly destroyed by Jesus.

Apostle
Apostle means 'one sent out' as a messenger or missionary. The word soon became an official title for Jesus' twelve disciples after his death and resurrection (Acts 1:25–6 and Ephesians 2:20).

As the Lord leads
This term is generally used when the person doesn't know what he or she should do in a particular situation.

Ascension
Forty days after his resurrection Jesus rose, 'ascended' into heaven to sit at the right hand of God.

Atonement
The work Jesus achieved through his life, death and resurrection that gave us new life.

Baptism
An outward sign of an inner commitment to Jesus. This is usually done by putting the person right under the water and bringing them straight back up again.

Bro'
Short for 'brother'. A term of endearment that is very useful if you forget the person's name.

Can I say something in love?
Generally means that the person wants to say something critical but thinks that prefixing their criticism with the above makes it all right.

Communion
Another term for Eucharist or the Lord's Supper. Through eating bread and drinking wine we remember Jesus' death and how much he loves us. Jesus commanded we should do this to remember him.

Conversion
The response to hearing the gospel, the good news of Jesus, and the conscious decision to believe, repent and follow him.

Death
The ending of our physical, bodily life. At the point of death, Christians immediately go into the presence of God.

Demons

Evil angels who rebelled against God and now attempt to wreak havoc in the world.

Doctrine

The Bible's views on a particular subject.

Ekklesia

The original Greek word for 'church'.

Eschatology

No, nothing to do with handcuffs or straitjackets. Eschatology is the study of the last days, i.e. the end of the world.

Eucharist

Another term for Communion or the Lord's Supper. Through eating bread and drinking wine we remember Jesus' death and how much he loves us. Jesus commanded we should do this to remember him.

Evangelism

Explaining the gospel message to unbelievers.

Faith

Trust in God.

Faith supper

A time when Christians all get together for something to eat. Instead of going out for a meal or dialling up a pizza or Chinese, this is a time when everyone brings something to eat and drink and everyone mucks in together. These are normally events where large amounts of quiche and flans and gallons of fruit juice are consumed.

Faithful word
Generally used after a sermon, when no one had the faintest idea what was being said, but wanted to make a positive comment.

Final judgment
The final judgment will take place after the millennium and it is Jesus' final decision on the ultimate destinies of everyone.

Gifts of the Holy Spirit
Gifts given by the Holy Spirit to help build the Church.

Giving thanks
Sometimes also called 'saying grace'. This is a (hopefully!) brief prayer of thanks for the food that is about to be consumed.

Glorification
This will happen after the second coming when Jesus raises the bodies of all Christians who have died and reunites them with their souls. At the same time Jesus will give all Christians still alive new, perfect, resurrected bodies, just like his own.

Going down in the Spirit
See also 'Slain in the Spirit'. Sometimes when the Holy Spirit is moving really powerfully, you literally fall to the floor for a short time. Our American friends sometimes call it 'carpet time' as the Holy Spirit refreshes you as you lie on the floor.

Great Commission
Jesus' final words to his earthly disciples before he ascended into heaven:

> Then Jesus came to them and said, 'All authority in heaven and on earth has been given to me. Therefore go and make disciples of all nations, baptising them in the name of the

Father and of the Son and of the Holy Spirit, and teaching them to obey everything I have commanded you. And surely I am with you always, to the very end of the age.'

(Matthew 28:18–20)

Heaven
The place where God lives. It is here where God reveals his glory and where angels, heavenly creatures and Christians all worship him.

Hell
A place of continued punishment for the wicked and those who have rejected Jesus.

Holy Spirit
One part of the Trinity who is left on the earth to do the will of God.

Incarnation
God coming in human form in the person of Jesus.

Inherited sin
Also called 'original sin'. The tendency for all to sin because we have inherited a sinful nature from Adam.

Laying a fleece
This is an interesting way to ask God for guidance. The idea of 'laying a fleece' comes from the pages of the Old Testament (Judges 6:36–40) where Gideon asked God for a sign by making a wool fleece damp with dew and the ground around it dry as a sign that he was hearing God correctly. These days, many Christians still ask God to do impossible things as a sign that he wants them to do something. You might say: 'Okay, God, I'll go to Africa next week if you send a Zulu warrior to my door at 3.36 p.m. on Monday, carrying a Lunn Poly holiday brochure

that falls open to the page with flight details to Zambia.'
Personally, I think 'fleeces' are to be avoided.

Let's lift Jill's leg up to the Lord
This peculiar phrase is often heard in prayer meetings. For 'Jill'
substitute the name of the person being prayed for, and for 'leg'
insert any other part of the human anatomy. Christians love to
see God healing people, but sometimes have a funny way of
asking him to do it.

Lord's Supper
Another term for Communion or Eucharist. Through eating
bread and drinking wine we remember Jesus' death and how
much he loves us. Jesus commanded we should do this to
remember him.

Mercy
God's kindness towards us.

Millennium
The one thousand-year period when Jesus will reign on earth.

New heaven and new earth
The brand new creation that Christians will live in after the
final judgment.

Omnipotence
One of the qualities of God. It means God is 'all-powerful'.

Omnipresence
One of the qualities of God. It means God is 'everywhere'.

Omniscience
One of the qualities of God. It means God is 'all-knowing'.

Original sin
Also called 'inherited sin'. The tendency for all to sin because we have inherited a sinful nature from Adam.

Postmillennialism
The view that Jesus will return to the earth after the millennium.

Premillennialism
The view that Jesus will return to earth before the millennium.

Pretribulational premillennialism
The view that Jesus will return secretly to earth before the tribulation to take all believers away (the Rapture), and then return again after the tribulation to reign on earth for a thousand years.

Prophecy
A gift of the Holy Spirit that involves speaking out something that God has brought to your mind.

Purgatory
A doctrine of the Roman Catholic Church that describes the place where the souls of believers go to have their sins purified from sin before they are allowed to enter heaven.

Rapture
The sudden taking up of believers to be with Jesus.

Repentance
Saying sorry and being sorry for our sins.

Sanctification
The work of God in our lives which makes us more like Jesus through our thoughts, words and actions.

Satan
The head of the demons. The Hebrew word *satan* means 'adversary' or 'accuser', and the equivalent Greek word is *diabolos* from which we get 'devil' and 'diabolical'.

Saved
Another way of saying that you're a Christian.

Scriptures
Another word for the Bible.

Second coming
The unexpected and very visual return of Jesus to the earth.

Sin
Everything we do, say and think that is wrong.

Slain in the Spirit
See also 'Going down in the Spirit'. Sometimes when the Holy Spirit is moving really powerfully, you literally fall to the floor for a short time. Our American friends sometimes call it 'carpet time' as the Holy Spirit refreshes you as you lie on the floor.

Speaking in tongues
A heavenly language to God. Often used during prayer or praise to God, tongues are words spoken, but not understood by the speaker.

Testimony
When used in Christian circles this word has nothing to do with giving a solemn statement in a court of law, so you can relax. When people 'share their testimony' they tell their own story of how they met Jesus. As a new Christian I heard and read many amazing accounts of how Satanists, drug addicts, criminals and Hell's Angels met Jesus and how their lives changed

overnight. Their stories always thrilled me but left me feeling rather inadequate as my own story seemed so ordinary. But the fact of the matter is that the average man or woman in the street isn't likely to be the high priest or priestess of an international witches' coven, and indeed are themselves pretty ordinary too. Your story of meeting Jesus is powerful as it is, so use it.

Transubstantiation

A doctrine of the Roman Catholic Church that teaches that the bread and wine used during Communion actually become the body and blood of Jesus.

Trinity

God exists as three persons, Father, Son and Holy Spirit.

Unforgivable sin

The deliberate and malicious rejection and slander of Jesus and the Holy Spirit. See Matthew 12:31–5 and Mark 3:29–30.

Vestry

Nothing to do with vests! This is a room in a church that is used for keeping the vestments – the traditional robes that ministers and vicars wear during traditional church services.

Bibliography

Anderson, Sir N., *Evidence for the Resurrection* (IVP, 1950)

Anderson, Sir N., *Jesus Christ: The Witness of History* (IVP, 1985)

Berkhof, L., *Introduction to Systematic Theology* (Eerdmans, 1932)

Briscoe, D.S., *Spirit Life* (Fleming H. Revell Co., 1960)

Bruce, F.F., *The Books and the Parchments* (Fleming H. Revell Co., 1950)

Bruce, F.F., *The New Testament Documents: Are They Reliable?* (IVP, 1960)

Chavda, M., *The Hidden Power of Prayer and Fasting* (Destiny Image, 1998)

Cho, P.Y., *Prayer: Key to Revival* (Word Books, 1984)

Erickson, M., *Christian Theology* (Baker, 1985)

Grieve, V., *Your Verdict* (IVP, 1988)

Halley, H.H., *Halley's Bible Handbook* (Zondervan, 2000)

Hosier, J., *The Lamb, the Beast and the Devil* (Monarch, 2002)

Huggett, J., *Listening to God* (Hodder & Stoughton, 1986)

Huggett, J., *Open to God* (Hodder & Stoughton, 2000)

John, J., *Your Kingdom Come* (Monarch, 2001)

Legg, S., *The A–Z of Evangelism* (Hodder & Stoughton, 2002)

Lewis, C.S., *Mere Christianity* (Fount, 1952)

Lucas, E., *Genesis Today* (Christian Impact, 2001)

McDowell, J., *Evidence that Demands a Verdict* (Campus Crusade, 1972)

McDowell, J., *More Evidence that Demands a Verdict* (Campus Crusade, 1975)

McDowell, J., *More than a Carpenter* (Kingsway, 1979)

McDowell, J., *The Resurrection Factor* (Campus Crusade, 1981)

McGrath, A.E., *Understanding Jesus* (Zondervan, 1987)

McGrath, A.E., *Christian Theology: An Introduction* (Blackwell, 1997)

Mallone, G., *Those Controversial Gifts* (Hodder Christian Books, 1993)

Maxwell, M., *Revelation* (Bible Reading Fellowship, 1997)

Morrison, F., *Who Moved the Stone?* (Faber, 1930)

Packer, J.I., *Concise Theology: A Guide to Historic Christian Beliefs* (Tyndale, 1993)

Pawson, D., *When Jesus Returns* (Hodder & Stoughton, 1995)

Phillips, J.B., *New Testament Christianity* (Hodder & Stoughton, 1958)

Robinson, J., *Can We Trust the New Testament?* (Mowbrays, 1977)

Stott, J.R.W., *The Cross of Christ* (IVP, 1986)

Tenney, T., *The God Chasers* (Destiny Image, 1998)

Tilby, A., *Son of God* (Hodder & Stoughton, 2001)

Tondeur, K., *Financial Tips for the Family* (Hodder & Stoughton, 1997)

Unger, F. and Larson, G.N., *The Hodder Bible Handbook* (Hodder & Stoughton, 1966)

Wangerin, W., *Paul – A Novel* (Lion, 2000)

Yancey, P., *The Jesus I Never Knew* (Marshall Pickering, 1995)

Young, J., *The Case Against Christ* (Hodder & Stoughton, 1986)

Breakout!

The Breakout Trust is a registered charity, committed to communicating the relevance of the Christian faith. Its Director is Steve Legg, a Christian speaker, entertainer and writer.

Through humour and fun, Steve attempts to smash the misconceptions that many have about Christianity, and to show how faith in Jesus is not only reasonable but very relevant and vitally important.

This he does in Britain and overseas in schools, colleges, universities, prisons and out on the streets. Face to face and through the medium of radio and television, he has reached millions across the world and seen thousands come to know the reality of the Christian faith for themselves.

Steve can be contacted at:

The Breakout Trust,
PO Box 3070,
Littlehampton
BN17 5WX

Tel: 01903 732 190
e-mail: steve@breakout.org.uk
or visit the website: www.breakout.org.uk